PURITY OF H

CW01335806

and

THE SEVEN SPIRITS

For hundreds of other excellent titles see:

www.**Classic***Christian***Ebooks**.com

Inspiring and uplifting classics from authors such as:

E. M. Bounds

Amy Carmichael

Alfred Edersheim

Jonathan Edwards

Charles Finney

D. L. Moody

G. Campbell Morgan

Andrew Murray

George Muller

Charles Spurgeon

Hudson Taylor

R. A. Torrey

John Wesley

...and many more!

A Division of:

DREAM Publishing International

TABLE OF CONTENTS

PURITY OF HEART

Letters to Salvation Army Officers

By

General William Booth

Preface

The following Letters were, in the first instance, addressed to weekly meetings of Salvation Soldiers. They called forth so many expressions of thankfulness, and so many requests that they might be printed in a permanent form, that I have gathered them together in this little book.

They do not, of course, profess to treat this great subject with anything like completeness, nor do I make any claim for them to literary elegance or power; and yet, if they are used at all, they must go as they are, for I have no opportunity to properly revise them.

William Booth

Chapter 1: Purity - What It Is

"Blessed are the pure in heart: for they shall see God."
- Matthew 5:8 -

My Dear Comrades,

We Salvationists are always singing or praying or talking about a Pure Heart. Indeed, there are few subjects of which we more frequently speak, or in which we more truly glory. Some of our most beautiful and heart-stirring songs are on this theme. Perhaps, no one is more frequently sung by us than that commencing,

"Oh for a heart to praise my God!
A heart from sin set free!
A heart that always feels the Blood,
So freely spilt for me!"

Is not that beautiful? But it goes on better still

"A heart in every thought renewed,
And full of Love Divine;
Perfect and right, and pure and good,
A copy, Lord, of Thine!"

Great, however, as is the power of such songs to stir our hearts, perhaps nothing delights the genuine Salvationist more than the definite testimonies of those living in the enjoyment of the Blessing, or the earnest prayers for its bestowment, or the fervent appeals to Comrades to secure this Pearl of Great Price, so often heard of in our ranks.

And yet I am afraid that many of our Soldiers do not definitely experience and openly profess the enjoyment of the Blessing; and I have been thinking that, perhaps, it is because the subject is not so well understood as it should be. I propose, therefore, to try to explain it in a few Letters, which I hope my Comrades will carefully consider.

Now, please remember that my subject is "Purity of Heart." I want to explain what we mean by a Pure Heart; to show how you may obtain the precious treasure, if you are not possessed of it already; and how you may keep the Blessing when attained. I will start off by saying:

We all know what is meant by being Pure. When we talk about the purity of things around us, we mean that they are clean and unadulterated. That is that they are not only without dirt or filthiness, but have no inferior substance mixed with them.

When we say that a man is pure, in the religious sense, we mean that he is right and honest and true inside and out; that he not only professes, but practices the things that have to do with his duty to God and man.

Sin is spoken of in the Bible as filthiness or defilement of the body, mind, or spirit. Purity in Religion must mean, therefore, the absence of such filthy things as drunkenness, gluttony, dishonesty, cheating, falsehood, pride, malice, bad tempers, selfishness, unbelief, disobedience, or the like. In short, to be pure in soul, signifies deliverance from all and everything which the Lord shows you to be opposed to His Holy Will. It means that you not only possess the ability to live the kind of life that He desires, but that you actually do live it.

Now, Purity, I need not tell you, my Comrades, is much admired and greatly desired by all right-minded beings. To begin with:

We all like material purity; for instance, I am sure that everyone reading this Letter prefers to have a clean body. When you rise in the morning, you are not comfortable till you have washed yourselves. When the miners come from the pit, or the farmers from the field, or the girls from the factory, their first demand is for water with which to cleanse themselves.

You like clean clothes and clean linen, do you not? Consider the money and labor that are expended in keeping your garments clean.

You like a clean home. See how the housewife scrubs and washes and brushes and dusts to keep the floor and windows and furniture clean.

You like a clean city. What a laborious and costly sweeping of the streets, and carrying away of rubbish there is; and what money is spent on the fixing and cleansing of sewers to keep our towns and cities sweet and pure.

We like this sort of purity, because it is pleasant to the eye and good for health. We know that dirt is hateful to the senses, breeds vermin, generates cholera, plague, and diseases in general, and hurries people to the grave. So we hate it, and say, "Away with it; let us be clean!"

But all right-minded beings admire the purity of the soul far more than they do the purity of the body, or the clothes, the home, or anything else; and that, because it is so much more important. For instance:

(a) God loves Soul Purity. It is His nature to do so. I have no doubt, like us He prefers to see His children outwardly clean. He tells us, through Paul, that we are to have our bodies washed with pure water; but the washing of the heart is far more desirable to Him than that of the body.

"His saints are lovely in His sight,
He views His children with delight;
He sees their hope, He knows their fear,
And looks, and loves His image there."

Yes, God delights in Holiness. Heaven, His dwelling place, is pure. Its inhabitants are pure. Its employments, and enjoyments, and worship are all alike pure.

(b) The Angels love Purity. If any unholy creature could, by any means, be introduced into the Celestial City, the inhabitants would, I am sure, avoid such a creature, as we should avoid a being who had some dreadful disease.

(c) The Devils know that Purity is a precious thing; although they hate it and oppose it with all their might.

(d) Many wicked men admire Purity. They look on it as being beautiful and desirable in others, although they regard it as being impossible to them. In their thoughtful moments, when the Spirit of God strives with them, when the recollections of the innocent days gone by crowd into their memories, and they see people who they know are clean and good, they hate themselves because of their own impurity, although all the time refusing to submit to God, and to accept the Salvation that would make them pure.

(e) Lost souls in Hell feel how infinitely superior Holiness is to Wickedness. They see now how much better it would have been for them if they had washed their hearts in the Blood of the Lamb when they had the privilege of doing so. Oh, what would they not give to have such opportunities as those enjoyed by you! Are you in love with Purity, my Comrades? Perhaps you possess it. Perhaps you have been to Jesus for the cleansing Power, laid yourselves at His feet, given up your doubtful things, offered yourselves to do His Will, living or dying, and believed that the Blood of Jesus Christ has made you clean.

Oh, if that experience has been yours, happy are you, and happier still if you are walking in the power and peace of that experience today. If it is so, I congratulate you; I delight in you, and praise God on your account.

But if this Blessing is not yours, are you longing after it? Does the thought of it fill your soul with desire? Does it make you feel like the poet, when he sang:

"O glorious hope of perfect love!
It lifts me up to things above,
It bears on eagles' wings;
It gives my ravished soul a taste,
And makes me for some moments feast
With Jesus' priests and kings."

Come along, my Comrades. Your happiness and your influence are all connected with your being made holy. Oh, I beseech you to kneel down here and now, and ask God to make you each and all pure, by the Power of the Holy Ghost, through the Blood of the Lamb.

Yours affectionately,

William Booth

Chapter 2: Purity Commanded

Follow...holiness, without which no man shall see the Lord.
- Hebrews 12:14 -

My Dear Comrades,

I want again to take up the subject on which I wrote in my last Letter. It is, indeed, a precious topic. I have loved it and talked about it all the way through my religious life; and, today, I regard the enjoyment and publication of the Blessing of a Clean Heart as being as essential to my own peace, power, and usefulness, and as necessary to the progress and prosperity of The Army as ever it was. Let me proceed, then, with the work of explanation. A right understanding of the subject will help you to obtain this Blessing for yourselves, and enable you to explain it to others.

In my last Letter I talked about Purity in general: in this I want to say something on the subject in its practical application to yourselves. What did our dear Lord mean when He spoke of the "Pure in Heart," and pronounced them blessed? What is it to have a Pure Heart? To answer that question, I must begin by asking another:

What is meant by the Heart? To which question I answer, we do not mean that organ which you can feel beating in your breast, and which is the central force of the bodily system. That is a very important part of a man, and the keeping of it in good condition is most essential.

But it is not the heart in your body to which Jesus Christ referred in this passage, and about which I want to talk to you; but that power which, being the central force of your soul, may be said to answer to it. As the heart which palpitates in your bosom is the great driving-force of the Natural Man, so the heart we are talking about is the great driving force of the Spiritual Man.

(a) In this sense it is your Heart that feels joy or sorrow. When you say, "That poor woman died of a broken heart on account of the ill-treatment of her husband," you mean that it was the bitter anguish of her soul which killed her.

(b) It is the Heart that chooses between right and wrong. When

11

you say, "My brother's heart is on the side of God, and goodness, and truth," you mean that these things are the supreme choice of his soul.

(c) It is the Heart that decides on the particular line of conduct to be pursued. When you say, "This young man went to the Mercy-Seat and gave his heart to God," you mean that he decided, in his inmost soul, to accept Salvation and become a Soldier of Christ.

(d) It is the Heart that loves righteousness and hates iniquity. When God says, "My son, give Me thy heart," He means "Come along, young man or woman, and love Me and holiness, and Souls, and hate the Devil and Sin, with all the powers you possess."

(e) It is the Heart that molds the character, guides the choice, and masters all the course and conduct of a man's life. The heart is the captain of the ship. It determines whether a man shall accept mercy, serve God, follow righteousness, live for the Salvation of his fellows, and finally enter the Heavenly Harbor in triumph, or whether he shall live a life of rebellion, die in his sins, and finish up a wreck on the rocks of everlasting despair. How important it is to each one of us that we should have a good - a right - a Pure Heart.

Now, seeing that the Heart is so thoroughly the master of the man, nothing can be much plainer, can it, my Comrades, than the necessity for that Heart being pure? But what is a Pure Heart? What is it to have a Heart that has been cleansed by the Power of the Holy Spirit through the Blood of Jesus Christ? That is a very important inquiry and I do hope that my dear Soldiers will give me their careful attention while I strive to answer it.

1. And first, a Pure Heart is not a Heart that is never Tempted to do evil Possibly there is no such thing in this world, nor ever has been, as a Non-Tempted Heart, that is, a man or a woman who has never been exposed to temptation to commit sin, of one kind or the other. Not only was our Blessed Lord tempted by the Devil in the wilderness, but He was beset with evil attractions all the way through His life. St. Paul expressly tells us that our Saviour was in all points tempted like as we are, but hallelujah! He effectually resisted the world, the flesh, and the devil, and came through the trying ordeal without a stain. He triumphed over all, for the Apostle exultingly assures us, that "He was without sin."

You will be tempted, my Comrades, all through your earthly journey, even to the very gates of Heaven; but, thank God, temptation is not sin, and Grace, abundant Grace, is provided to enable you to triumph over all the fascinations of earth and all the devices of hell. You can come off more than conqueror. But, remember, although you may have a Pure Heart you will have to fight temptation.

2. A Pure Heart is not a Heart that cannot suffer. Beyond question, Jesus Christ had a Pure Heart; He was Holy and undefiled, and yet He was "The Man of Sorrows." Paul tells us that although he exercised himself to have always a conscience void of offense towards God and towards man, yet was he not saved from being, at times, "in heaviness through manifold temptations."

All the Saints of old had hours of darkness and depression, many of them going through seas of anguish. And as with the Saints of old, so is it with the Saints of modern times. It is not sinful to weep and be cast down, if in our distress we do not give way to unbelief and despair and wrong-doing. Cheer up, brothers and sisters! "By floods and flames surrounded," you must "still your way pursue." If you keep believing you will not be confounded; God will deliver you.

3. By a Pure Heart we do not mean a Heart that cannot sin. The Devil was once a beautiful, sinless creature. But he yielded to temptation. The sinless crown fell from his beautiful brow, and from a pure archangel he was changed into a foul fiend, and hurled all the way from his bright and sinless Heaven to his dark and gloomy hell. Adam was pure when he came from the hands of his Maker. God pronounced him to be good; but, led away by Satan, he lost his Purity, and was cast out of Eden into a world of sin and sorrow and death.

Alas! alas! we have the unspeakable sorrow of too frequently seeing Saints and Soldiers fall from Holiness into sin. Some of the many miserable Backsliders around us once walked closely with God, kept their garments unspotted from the world, and were examples of all that is pure and good. But they have gone back to the beggarly elements of the world, and, like the sow that was washed, they are again wallowing in the mire.

So, my Comrades, you will see that no matter however pure you may become, it will be possible for you to sin. Though you wash your garments white, and for a season walk with God in holy communion, and have Faith so that you can remove mountains and save multitudes, you must remember that while you are in this life it is possible for you to fall from Grace. Nay, you must remember that unless you take heed to yourselves, and watch and pray, the probabilities are that you will be overtaken by some besetting sin, and, after having saved others, become yourself a castaway. Therefore, "let him that thinketh he standeth take heed lest he fall."

4. By a Pure Heart, we do not mean any experience of Purity, however blessed it may be, that cannot increase in enjoyment, usefulness, and power. Pull the weeds out of your garden, and the flowers and plants and trees will grow faster, flourish more abundantly, and become more fruitful.

Just so, this very moment, let Jesus Christ purge the garden of your souls of envy and pride, and remove the poisonous plants of malice and selfishness and every other evil thing, and Faith and peace, and hope and love, and humility and courage, and all the other beautiful flowers of Paradise will flourish in more charming beauty and more abundant fruitfulness.

Oh, will you not go down now before God, and give yourselves fully over into the hands of your precious Saviour? He is waiting to sanctify you. Cast overboard all that hinders. It is God that purifies the Heart. Will you let Him do the work? Now cry out in Faith: "Anger and sloth, desire and pride, This moment be subdued; Be cast into the crimson tide Of my Redeemer's Blood."

But you must go a little further, my Comrades, and, boldly and believingly, sing that song of triumph:

'Tis done, Thou dost this moment save,
With full Salvation bless;
Redemption through Thy Blood I have,
And spotless love and peace."

Yours affectionately,
William Booth

"Come, Holy Ghost, all Sacred Fire,
Come, fill Thy earthly temples now;
Emptied of every base desire,
Reign Thou within, and only Thou.

"Thy sovereign right, Thy gracious claim
To every thought and every power;
Our lives to glorify Thy name,
We yield Thee in this sacred hour.

"Fill every chamber of the soul;
Fill all our thoughts, our passions fill,
Till under Thy supreme control
Submissive rests our cheerful will.

'Tis done! Thou dost this moment come,
My longing soul is all Thine own;
My heart is Thy abiding home.
Henceforth I live for Thee alone."

Chapter 3: Purity Means Deliverance

That He would grant unto us, that we...might serve Him without fears in holiness and righteousness before Him, all the days of our life.
- Luke 1:74-75 -

My Dear Comrades,

I hope that I shall not weary you by returning again to the question of "A Pure Heart." The subject is so important to the whole Christian Church, to the entire Salvation Army, nay, to the wide, wide world, that it must be lifted up. Holiness has been so great a blessing to us in the past, and will, I am sure, be so much greater a blessing to us in the future, that I feel that it must be brought to the front.

You must see its value, and understand its meaning. If you are not living in the enjoyment of the peace, power, and gladness of Holiness, it is, possibly, because you entertain some mistaken notions respecting it. The ability of the Devil to lead people astray on this, as on many other questions, is largely in proportion to his power to deceive them. Can I better make you understand what is meant by Purity of Heart?

You will remember that in my last Letter I tried to show you that by a Pure Heart we did not mean a heart that could not, or would not, be tempted, or that could not, or would not, be called to suffer; nor that the Soldier out of whose heart all impurity had been expelled could not sin, or would have reached such a state of experience beyond which he would not be able to grow in faith, and hope, and charity, and in all the Graces of the Holy Spirit.

What, then, is a Pure Heart? I reply that a Pure Heart is a heart that has been cleansed by the Holy Spirit from all sin, and enabled to please God in all it does; to love Him with all its powers, and its neighbor as itself. Where this experience is enjoyed by anyone it may be said that God has made the heart Pure, even as He is Pure.

But here I may be asked the question, "Does not God bestow this wonderful deliverance from sin on the soul at conversion? Does He not sanctify and make it good and holy at the same time that He pardons its sins?" No, I reply; although a great work is done for the soul at conversion, its deliverance from sin at that time is not complete. It is true, that He does a great deal for a man when He makes that remarkable change. He destroys the bondage in which sin holds the transgressor; but the destruction of sin out of the heart and out of the life is not entire. Here let me try and show you the difference in the purification that comes to a man when he is fully cleansed. I will do this by setting forth the three different states into which the soul can come with respect to sin:

1. Before a man or a woman is converted, some particular sin is the master of the soul. That is, some unlawful appetite or selfish passion always rules the individual, and makes him act as it dictates.

What do I mean by sin being the master? I answer that the unconverted soul is held by it in a bondage from which it cannot get away. It has no choice. It is under its power. It must sin. The soul may have light to see its evil and ruinous character. It may hate it, struggle against it, make resolutions never to do it again. But it is driven, by its own nature, to do the things that it does not want to do; and is prevented from doing the things that it wishes to do, often, as the Apostle describes, crying out in bitterness of spirit, as it struggles and fights with it, "O wretched man that I am! Who shall deliver me from this wretched condition of slavery that is worse than death?"

This is the experience of every unsaved man and woman; at least of everyone who has light to see what an evil thing sin is. It is true, that the character of the mastering sin will differ in different persons. In some people the governing evil may be something that is looked upon by the world as vulgar, such as drunkenness, or lust, or dishonesty, or gambling, or some other evil passion that has gotten hold of the sinner, and from which he cannot get away, and for which every precious thing on earth and in Heaven is sacrificed. In other cases, it may be some sin that is not so much despised by what is called the respectable part of the community, such as pride, ambition, selfishness, secret infidelity or the like. But, in some form or other, sin rules in the heart of every ungodly man. He is mastered by sin.

2. Now, let us look at the Second State into which a man can come with respect to Sin. When he is saved, not only does he receive the pardon of sin, but deliverance from its bondage. The yoke is broken, the fetters are snapped, the prison doors are opened, he is free! Instead of sin being his master, he is the master of sin. Instead of drink, or temper, or money-worship, or worldly pleasure, or some

other devilish thing driving him down the broad way to destruction, against his judgment, against his own wishes, against the strivings of the Spirit, he is made free to do the Will of God and to climb the narrow way to Heaven.

But, great and glorious as is the change wrought in the heart at conversion, maybe deliverance is not complete. The power of sin is broken, but there are still certain evil tendencies left in the soul. There are what the Apostle terms "the roots of bitterness." These evils ordinarily grow and increase in power, involving the soul in constant conflict, and as the time goes by, often gain the mastery, and as the result, there is much sinning and repenting.

3. Then comes the Third State. Tired of this conflict, hating these internal evils, weeping over the pride and malice, and envy and selfishness, that the soul still finds within, it rises up, and cries out:

"Tell me what to do to be pure,
In the sight of the All-seeing eyes?
Tell me, is there no thorough cure,
No escape from the sins I despise?
Tell me, can I never be free
From this terrible bondage within?
Is there no deliverance for me?
Must I always have sin dwell within?"

To this question God sends the glad answer back: "Then will I sprinkle clean water upon you, and ye shall be clean: from all your filthiness, and from all your idols, will I cleanse you. A new heart also will I give you, and a new spirit will I put within you; and I will take away the stony heart out of your flesh, and I will give you an heart of flesh. And I will put My Spirit within you, and cause you to walk in My statutes, and ye shall keep My judgments, and do them."

"All things are possible to him that believeth." Then the soul believes, the sanctifying Spirit falls, and the Third Stage is reached - which is Salvation from all sin. In the First stage the Soul is Under Sin. In the Second stage the Soul is Over Sin. In the Third stage the Soul is Without Sin.

In which stage are you, my Comrades? Settle it for yourselves. Have you got a Pure Heart? Examine yourselves. What is your reply?

Some of you in describing your experience can adopt the words

18

of the Apostle, with a little variation, and say: The very God of peace has sanctified me wholly: and He preserves my whole spirit and soul and body blameless, and He will continue to do so unto the coming of our Lord Jesus Christ. Faithful is He that has called me to this experience of Purity, who also will do it.

All glory to God, my Comrades. Give Him all the praise. Be careful to "walk in the light, as He is in the light," then shall you have fellowship with Him and with other sanctified souls, and the Blood of Jesus Christ His Son shall keep you cleansed from all sin. In which case He will use you to promote His glory, make you useful, and show you still greater things.

To those who know that they do not possess a Pure Heart, I put the question, Will you have one now?

God is waiting to cleanse you. What doth hinder your receiving the purifying Baptism? "Now is the accepted time." Tell God that all the doubtful things shall be given up, and then go down before Him, singing while you kneel:

"Faith, mighty faith, the promise sees,
And looks to that alone,
Laughs at impossibilities,
And cries, 'It now is done.'"

Yours affectionately,

William Booth

Chapter 4: Purity Described

Now the God of peace, that brought again from the dead our Lord Jesus...through the blood of the everlasting covenant, make you perfect in every good work to do His will working in you that which is well-pleasing in His sight, through Jesus Christ; to whom be glory for ever and ever. Amen.
- Hebrews 13:20-21 -

My Dear Comrades,

Has anything I have said set anyone among you longing after the possession of the precious, the inestimable, Blessing of a Pure Heart? Has anyone in your Corps been heard singing:

"Oh, when shall my soul find her rest,
My strugglings and wrestlings be o'er;
My heart, by my Saviour possessed,
Be fearing and sinning no more?"

It is those who "hunger and thirst after righteousness" that are to be "filled." If this desire has been created, in any degree, I am delighted. Let me try and increase that longing, by holding up before your eyes some of the advantages that flow out of the possession of the Blessing. And the first thing I mention that seems calculated to create this desire is the fact that,

1. A Pure Heart will ensure a Holy Life. But here does anyone who has not heard my previous explanation of this subject ask, "What do I mean by a holy life?" I answer, that it is a life that meets the requirements, and ensures the fulfillment of the promises of this Holy Book; a life fashioned after the life of the Lord Jesus Christ. It will, at the best, be very imperfect, have many weaknesses about it, and be subjected to many mistakes; but still, according to the light possessed, it will be a holy life.

Is not such a life desirable, my Comrades? Is not a man who is able to live out his religion before his family, before his workmates, and before the world, highly privileged? Will he not be a means of blessing to those around him, whichever way he turns? Look at him.

He is honest and faithful in all his worldly dealings, in his shop, factory, home, or wherever he may come. He has an honest heart.

He is true to his promises and engagements. His word is his bond. You can trust him either in or out of sight. He has a true heart.

He is industrious. He neither shirks his duty, nor wastes his time, nor scamps his work. He has an industrious heart.

He is kind. He is loving to his wife, tender to his children, faithful to his comrades, considerate for his servants, gentle to the weak, sympathetic to the sick. He has a kind heart.

He is compassionate. He pities the poor, yearns over the Backslider, fights for the Salvation of sinners in public, and cries to God for their deliverance in private. He has a soul-loving heart.

He is a holy man. His secret life is holy. In thought and feeling, conversation and disposition, he is able to please God and do His blessed Will. He has a Pure Heart. Is not such a heart desirable, my Comrades? I thank God for as many of you as have been brought, by Divine Grace, into the possession of this beautiful treasure, but I want you all to come up to this standard. I want you all to enter this holy state.

2. But, further, a Pure Heart will give you Peace. It is a condition of peace. You cannot have peace without it. I am always saying to you, in one form or another, that you must not expect a life of uninterrupted gladness in this world. It cannot be. Our imperfect bodies, with all their pains and weaknesses; the temptations of the Devil, and the miseries of a world in rebellion against God, prevent anything like a life of unmixed rejoicing for you and me.

But peace, "the peace of God, the peace that passeth all understanding," is your birthright, and with a Pure Heart, the treasure shall be yours. I say again, that while you are here you must have certain strife. You cannot help it. You will have strife with the Devil. War to the knife with hell. You will have strife with wicked men. They will fight you because you are for righteousness and God, and for the deliverance of men from their power.

But, Hallelujah! in the heart that is purified by the Holy Spirit, and sprinkled with the Blood of the Lamb, the strife with God has ceased, the war with conscience is ended, the fear of death and hell is over. The soul possessed of a Pure Heart has entered "the rest that remaineth to the people of God."

Do you enjoy this rest, my Comrades? Is the inward strife over? Oh, make haste, and let the Blessed Spirit, who waits to sanctify you wholly, cast out the enemies of your soul!

It is not your poverties, nor your persecutions, nor your afflictions, nor your ignorances, nor ever so many other things all put together, that prevent your perfect peace. Sin is the enemy; and when malice and indolence, and ambition and unbelief, and every other evil thing has been cast out, your "peace shall flow as a river, and your righteousness shall abound as the waves of the sea."

3. Purity of Heart is the condition on which God will enter and dwell in your soul. Now listen, my Comrades, and cry to God for an increase of Faith, seeing that what I am going to say is a great mystery. But it is, nevertheless, gloriously true. God wants to live with you, not only in your home, but in your very heart. Poor and ignorant as you may be among men, and little noticed, nay, even despised, by the great and rich people of the world, yet God - the great God, whom the "heaven of heavens cannot contain" - wants to come and live in your heart and that not as a visitor only, but as an abiding guest.

An old writer curiously says, "God is like the rich people in one respect. He has two houses - a town house and a country house. His town house is in the Celestial City, but His country house is in the hearts of His people." Hear what He says Himself: "For thus saith the high and lofty One that inhabiteth eternity, whose name is Holy; I dwell in the high and holy place" and "with him also that is of a contrite and humble spirit" in order "to revive the spirit of the humble, and to revive the heart of the contrite ones."

Brother, sister, can you not hear Him saying, "Behold, I stand at the door and knock: if any man hear My voice, and open the door, I will come in to him"?

"O joyful sound of gospel grace!
Christ shall in me appear;
I, even I, shall see His face;
I shall be holy here.

"This heart shall be His constant home;
I hear His Spirit cry;
'Surely,' He saith, 'I quickly come';
He saith who cannot lie."

Will you not say "Amen, come in, Lord Jesus, and come quickly?" Will you not let all go that would prevent Him entering?

Will you not fling the gates of your soul wide open, and let Him come in? If you will, go down before Him just now, and bid Him welcome.

I have much more to say to you on this precious subject, but it must wait till another time. Meanwhile, wait no longer for a full Salvation.

Yours affectionately,

William Booth

"Jesus, my All-in-all Thou art,
My rest in toil, my ease in pain,
The medicine of my broken heart,
In war my peace, in loss my gain,
In grief my joy unspeakable,
My life in death, my All-in-all.
In want my plentiful supply,
In weakness my almighty power,
In bonds my perfect liberty,
My light in Satan's darkest hour,
In grief my joy unspeakable,
My life in death, my heaven in hell."

Chapter 5: Purity And Love

*But now being made free from sin, and become servants to God, ye have
your fruit unto holiness, and the end everlasting life.*
- Romans 6:22 -

My Dear Comrades,

Since writing my last Letter, I have been visiting the
Salvationists of Switzerland, Italy, and France. Everywhere I find
vast openings for The Salvation Army. Everywhere I have met with
dear Comrades longing to make the most of their opportunities; and
everywhere, it has seemed to me, that more Red-hot Religion would
make these Comrades equal to the splendid chances of usefulness
that lie right before them.

But is it not the same in Great Britain, America, Australia, and
in every other part of the world to which these Letters will come? Is
it not so in your Corps? - nay, is it not so with every individual
Soldier who reads these words?

Now, as I have explained to you before, by Red-hot Religion I
mean hearts made hot with love for God, for Comrades, for
perishing souls, for noble work, and for every other good thing
possible to men or women on earth or in Heaven. I mean hearts
made hot with holy love, such love as will compel us to toil and
sacrifice for the welfare of the object cared for. Such love as will
make its possessor the servant of those beloved, and exercise a self-
denying mastery over the heart that experiences it. Such love will be
like our Master's. For "herein is love, not that we loved God, but that
He loved us."

Look at the Mother's love. Does it not make her sacrifice time,
comfort, and health for her child?

Look at the Patriot's love. Does it not compel him to turn his
back on home, family, business, to fight and die for his country?

And so Hot love in the Salvationist will make him lay health,
time, goods, and all he possesses at the Feet of his Lord, and there
use all in blessing and saving the souls of men.

Now it is this spirit of Love which makes this blessed heat in the
souls of men and women. As the Devil lights and feeds the fires of

malice, ambition, selfishness, pride, lust, and the other evils that encourage and strengthen souls in their warfare with God, and carries them down the broad way to destruction, so the fierce heat of Pure Love, created and maintained by the Holy Spirit, makes the Salvationist watch and pray, toil and talk and suffer, careless of what it costs him in doing so, if he can thereby gain the blessed object on which his heart is set.

But the Holy Spirit only dwells, in all His mastering power and burning zeal, in souls that have been cleansed from evil; so that if you are resolved to spend your life in blessing and saving men, and fighting for your Lord, you must have a Pure Heart.

A Pure Heart will make you a blessing to those around you, and that not merely as a result of what you do, but from the fact of what you are. People will, no doubt, be drawn to love Christ, and seek Salvation, and fight for The Army by what you say and sing. Your appeals and your prayers will all affect them; but if, in addition, you possess this treasure they will also be led to God and Holiness and Heaven by what they see you are.

A Pure Heart, as we have seen, makes a good life. Goodness is attractive; men respect it, and are drawn to it, for what it is in itself. Even if they are themselves the slaves of what is bad and devilish, they cannot help admiring what is Holy and Divine. And if this is the case with the slaves of sin and vice, it will be a thousand times more so with those around you who have already been captivated by the charms of Holiness. To such hearts, your life, if governed and inspired by Pure Love, will be a constant source of light, and strength, and consolation.

This is what we call Influence. It is something that is always going on. It is like the fragrance of a rose. You take the flower and place it in the middle of a room, and day and night it will send forth a sweet smell to all around. You have not to do anything at it, or with it. You need not wave it about, or pass it from one to another. It will spread abroad its pleasant perfume quite apart from any movement.

So it is with the Soldier who enjoys Purity of Heart, and lives in harmony with the experience. A holy influence will be going out from him all the time, not only from what he says and does, but from what he is himself.

You feel the power, and the sweetness, and the genuineness of his spirit and devotion. And when you hear his testimony, or listen to his prayers, or hear his pleading with sinners, you feel this blessed influence proceeding from him wherever you find him.

As you look into his eyes, and shake his hand, or sit by his side, it will be there. When you see him in the furnace of affliction, or stand by his dying bed, or follow him to the grave; nay, long after he has passed from mortal sight, this influence will continue to flow out to you. For years to come, a sight of his photograph or the bare mention of his name, will warm your heart, strengthen your courage, sustain your faith, and increase your love for all that is Christlike and true. Why is this, my Comrades? It is because you believed he was a Holy man. You admired his self-sacrificing life. You felt that he had a Pure Heart.

There is another inducement which should lead you to seek a Pure Heart, and that is, because it will bring you into the possession of a good hope. This is a precious treasure. To feel that whatever clouds may darken the sky, or whatever sorrows may sweep over your soul, there is good ground for anticipating peace, and joy and victory in the future, must be a precious and desirable thing.

A Soldier who knows that he sincerely loves God, and that he is living in obedience to Him, has an inward assurance that God will care for him, whatever troubles may arise. Whereas one who feels that he has malice, hatred, pride, love of the world, and other wrongs hidden away in his secret soul, and who knows that he is daily neglecting his duty to his family or to himself, to his Corps, or the poor sinners around him, can no more have a bright hope that God is going to make him a happy future, than the sinners can expect that they are going to have Heaven at the end of a sinful life. He may hope for it, but it will be like the hope of the hypocrite, certain to be destroyed.

But when the soul has the witness of the Spirit and of a consistent life, to the possession of inward Purity, it can look forward with confidence to victory over every foe, deliverance out of every sorrow, and in the end, glory and honor, immortality and eternal life.

Have these blessed experiences any charm for you, my Comrades? Let me review them. I think they are entrancing.

1. There is the Holy Life that will always be the outcome of a Holy Heart. If the fountain spring is pure, the flowing waters of

daily life and action will be pure also.

2. There is the peace of God that passeth all understanding, which is ever associated with inward Holiness. "The wicked are like the troubled sea, when it cannot rest, whose waters cast up mire and dirt." Any evil left in the soul must make trouble. Purity and Peace are bound together by God Himself.

3. There is the presence and the indwelling of God as a flame of Holy Love, which is the strength and spirit of Holiness. This is the Fiery Baptism which burns up hatred, and grudges, and self-seeking, and self-will, and purifies all our motives and affections.

4. There is the useful life and the Holy Example that flow from a Pure Heart, which will not only speak in favor of God and Holiness while you live, but shall go on influencing the world long after you have passed to your reward in the skies.

5. There is a blooming hope of the future and the brightness of your crown in Eternity. The realization of all this glorious experience, my Comrades, hangs on your possession of a Pure Heart. These are only some of the inestimable blessings that flow out of this eternal spring of purity and power. Have you got this treasure? If so, Hallelujah! If not, I want you to go down and Seek it now.

Yours affectionately,

William Booth

"Love surpassing understanding,
Angels would the mystery scan,
Yet so tender that it reaches
To the lowest child of man.
Let me, Jesus,
Fuller know redemption's plan.

"Love that pardons past transgression,
Love that cleanses every stain,
Love that fills to overflowing,
Yet invites to drink again,
Precious fountain!
Which to open, Christ was slain.

"From my soul break every fetter,
Thee to know is all my cry;
Saviour, I am Thine forever,
Thine I'll live, and Thine I'll die.
Only asking,
More and more of love's supply."

Chapter 6: Purity Possible

Wherefore Jesus also, that He might sanctify the people with His own blood, suffered without the gate.
- Hebrews 13:12 -

My Dear Comrades,

I can very well imagine that some of my Soldiers, after reading what I have been saying about a Pure Heart, will be asking the question: "Is it possible for me to obtain this treasure?"

I am aware that many people outside our borders openly assert that such an experience is impossible. They declare that no man or woman can live in this world without committing sin. They say that no matter how we hate our sins, or weep over them, or pray to be delivered from them, or trust in Jesus Christ for victory over them, we must be beaten in the strife and go on sinning, or, at the best, keep on sinning and repenting, right down to the River of Death.

Now, with regard to this objection, I maintain with the Apostle John, that not only is God willing and able to forgive us our sins - which no one who believes the Bible will deny - but that He is equally willing and able to cleanse us from all unrighteousness.

But before we go further, let us have another word of explanation. We must understand one another. What is it that I am saying? I reply, I am declaring to you who hear these words, nothing less than the Scriptural doctrine that God can keep you from committing sin.

Perhaps some of you will ask, What is Sin? I reply that the same Apostle, that is John, answers that question in such a simple manner that anyone can understand him. He says in his Epistle, that "All unrighteousness is sin." That is, whatsoever thing a man does, or consents to being done, in his thoughts, desires, or actions, which he knows to be wrong, that is sin. Now I affirm, on the authority of the Bible, that Jesus Christ your Saviour is able and willing to keep you from doing wrong. His Name was called Jesus, that is, Saviour, because He "should save His people from their sins."

As I have shown you already in these Letters, you may make mistakes; you may have temptations; you may be low-spirited; you may have pain in your body, perplexity in your mind, and anguish in your heart; the world may be against you; dark clouds may hang low, and the future be threatening; nay, you may, like Jesus Christ on the Cross, even feel as though God and man had forsaken you, and yet, in spite of all this and all else of the same kind, you can be kept from sin. In the name of my dear Lord, I assert that it is possible for you to have and to keep a Pure Heart.

Many of you believe this already - and are as sure of it as I am myself. But some may be in doubt. Let me try and make it plain to them. 1. First, you cannot doubt God's Ability to make and keep you free from Sin. He who made you, and sustains you in being, who redeemed you on the Cross, who pardoned your sins, and wrote your name in Heaven, can surely do this for you. He who will raise you from the dead, and land you at last safely in Heaven, is surely able to keep you from breaking His commandments and grieving His Holy Spirit all the rest of the short time you may have to spend in this world! I am sure He can.

It will be a difficult task, perhaps, fixed as you are, with your particular trials of body and soul, or circumstances. There may be something in your family or your business very strongly opposed to your leading a holy life. You may have tried before, again and again, but only to fail. You may be full of doubts and fears, even to despair, and nothing short of a great Salvation will meet your case. But God will be equal to the undertaking. I am sure He will. He has saved you from many sins already. Evil habits and passions, that used to reign over you, have been mastered; nay, some of them have been destroyed. Why, then, should not your prayer be answered?

"Finish, then, Thy new Creation, Pure and spotless let me be;
Let me see Thy great Salvation, Perfectly restored in Thee."

I see no reason why He should not do this. He is able to keep the Angels from sinning. They do not keep themselves. It is His almighty arm that holds them up and prevents them from falling.

He will be able to keep you from sinning when you reach the Celestial Land; and, thank God, He can keep you here. You believe He is mighty to save. You sing, and sing, and sing again:

"All things are possible to him, That can in Jesus' name believe;
Lord, I no more Thy truth blaspheme,
Thy truth I lovingly receive;
I can, I do believe in Thee, All things are possible to me."

2. And then my Comrades, if God is able to make and keep you Pure, you cannot question His willingness to do it. This must be equally plain to you, and yet it will bear looking at. It is very important indeed, that you should see - yes, and feel as well - that Jesus Christ is not only able, but perfectly willing - nay, waiting - even while this is being read to you, to take away from your hearts the evil things that have been the plague of your lives, and for ever to keep them from coming back to harass, and wound, and torment you again.

(a) The very Nature of God proves His willingness to make you Holy. All beings everywhere act out their nature. You see illustrations of this around you every day - wicked people delight in the wickedness of their neighbors. Good people find pleasure in their goodness. God is Holy. He tells us so, again and again; and being Holy and hating iniquity, He must abhor wickedness in men and women, and find the great delight of His heart in making them pure and good like Himself. I am sure that nothing would gratify Him more, my Comrades, than to take everything that is unclean out of your hearts and lives. Will you let Him do it?

(b) God tells us, in plain language, in the Bible, that He wants to make you Holy. Listen to some of His words: "Put on the new man," He says, "which after God is created in righteousness and true holiness." "Be ye therefore perfect, even as your Father in Heaven is perfect." "For God hath not called us unto uncleanness, but unto Holiness." "This is the will of God, even your Sanctification."

3. Jesus Christ came into the world and lived and suffered and died that you might be made Holy. This was the main object of His life and death and resurrection. "For this purpose the Son of God was manifested, that He might destroy the works of the devil." Paul says that "Jesus gave Himself for His church" - that is, for you and for me - "that He might sanctify and cleanse us, and that He might present us to Himself...not having spot, or wrinkle, or any such thing; but that we should be holy, and without blemish."

4. His love for His Children proves His willingness to save them from their sins. No miser ever loved his gold; no patriot ever loved his country; no mother ever loved her babe; no father ever loved his boy; no bridegroom ever loved his bride; no, not all the love of all the created beings on this earth put together would equal the love which God bears to you, His children, my dear Comrades. And knowing as He does, that sin is your great curse, He must, nay, He

does, long to deliver you from it.

5. God has promised you a Clean Heart if you will seek it. "Wherefore come out from among them, and be ye separate, saith the Lord, and touch not the unclean thing; and I will receive you, and will be a Father unto you, and ye shall be My sons and daughters, saith the Lord Almighty."

6. But I am also sure that God is willing to give you a Clean Heart because He has done the work for so many of His servants in the days gone by, and for so many of your Comrades in our present time. He is no respecter of persons. You are as welcome to wash away your inward iniquities, in the fountain opened for sin and uncleanness, as any other son or daughter of Adam. Oh, He Will be delighted for you to step into the blessed stream at once:

"Will you, will you now enter in?
Will you, will you wash and be clean?"

7. If you are a Holy Man or Woman you will help forward the War, and spread the glory of Christ's Name far more effectively than you will if you are not fully saved. Holy people are the great need of the world. I am sure they are one of the great wants of The Army.

8. Do you not feel in your heart, while I am talking to you, that the Holy Spirit wants you to be Pure, and is waiting now to give you the Blessing? The fire of desire for your Sanctification is burning strongly in my heart while I write this Letter. Does not your desire also rise up for this? I believe it does. Well, wait no longer! All things are now ready! Is not a holy yearning springing up within you? Go down this moment before God, and sing:

"Oh, that the Fire from Heaven might fall,
And all my sins consume!
Come, Holy Ghost, for Thee I call,
Spirit of Burning, come!
"Refining Fire, go through my heart,
Illuminate my soul;
Scatter Thy life through every part,
And sanctify the whole."

Yours affectionately,

William Booth

"More hard than marble is my heart,
And foul with sins of deepest stain;
But Thou the mighty Saviour art,
Nor flowed Thy cleansing Blood in vain;
Ah, soften, melt this rock, and may
Thy Blood wash all these stains away!

"O grant that nothing in my soul
May dwell, but Thy pure love alone;
O may Thy love possess me whole,
My joy, my treasure, and my crown!
Strange flames far from my heart remove;
My every act, word, thought, be love."

Chapter 7: Purity, God's Gift

But we have this treasure in earthen vessels, that the excellency of the
power may be of God, and not of us.
- 2 Corinthians 4:7 -

My Dear Comrades,

I now come to one of the most important parts of this very interesting subject.

"How can a Pure Heart be obtained?" I think I hear you say, "It is good, very precious, very desirable; oh, how I wish the treasure was mine! But how can I get it?"

Now, here I think it will be profitable for us to have a look back over the road we have traveled together while considering this blessed experience. And first of all, you will remember that I tried to show you what Holiness was. I begged you not to set it too high, as continued rapture or an every-hour hallelujah feeling. Then, I cautioned you against setting it too low - that is, regarding it as being consistent with anything like the commission of actual sin. Then I showed you how valuable the Blessing would be to you, because it meant peace and usefulness, and the continued smile of God. Then I went on to explain that it was a possible experience, maintaining that, no matter whether rich or poor, young or old, married or single, God could cleanse you from all filthiness of the flesh and of the spirit, and enable you to be perfect in Holiness before Him all the days of your life. I come now to answer what I hope is the cry of many hearts, "How can I find this Pearl of Great Price?"

Now you ask - "What must I do to be Pure?" and in reply I say that there is certainly something to be done, and something that you will have to do yourselves. To understand what that something is, you must keep well before your minds the fact that there are two forces or powers that have to unite in the Purification of the Heart.

The first is the Divine - that is, God.

The second is the human - that is, man, which means yourself.

God and man are partners in the transaction. This is nothing new; it is the same in the affairs of your every-day life. You use the natural abilities God has given you to buy and sell, and plow and plant: and, as the result, God gives you food and raiment. This was the case when you were converted; you repented and believed, and God saved your soul. It will be the same when you are sanctified. The great work of cleansing your heart, and keeping it clean, will be performed by God Himself; but there will be some conditions which you will have to fulfill on your part.

From first to last it is "God that saves." Fix your mind well on that truth. If ever you have a Pure Heart, it will come from God's own Hand. When Jonah arrived definitely at the belief that Salvation was of the Lord, and trusted Him for it, his deliverance was nigh; for we read that immediately the Lord spake unto the fish, and it vomited him on to the dry land.

Only God can take out of your heart the bad temper, pride, malice, revenge, love of the world, and all the other evil things that have taken possession of it, and fill it with holy love and peace. To God you must look - to God you must go. This is the work of the Holy Ghost; He is the Purifying Fire; He is the Cleansing Flame; He only can sprinkle you with the water that purges the dross and takes away the sin; He only can make and keep you clean. What a blessing it is you have a God who is not only so mighty, but so willing to save!

"Yourself you cannot save,
Yourself you cannot keep;
But strength in Him, you surely have,
Whose eyelids never sleep."

But then, as I have said, there is something to be done on your side, and the chief part of that something is the exercise of Faith. The Apostles, met in council at Jerusalem, affirmed that God purifies the heart by Faith. That is to say, where the soul comes to God, and offers itself to Him for the doing of all His sacred Will, and believes that, for the sake of Jesus Christ, He does then and there cleanse it from all sin, that moment the Spirit answers to the Faith, the work of Purity is done and the soul can sing:

"He tells me when, and where, and how,
Just at His footstool as I bow;
The Blood of Jesus cleanses now,
This moment I believe."

You will see, then, that

1. This Purification is not effected by any human power. No priest or Officer can by his own force cleanse your heart. We can help one another by our example, by our testimony, by our exhortations, by our advice. There is not a Soldier here who, if he will yield himself up to God, and trust Him for full deliverance, will not at once receive power to bless and save those around him as never before. But no Comrade has the power to reach in to the heart of a Comrade, and cleanse it from the evil it finds there; that is the work of Jesus Christ alone. He can touch you this very moment with His loving bloodstained Hand, and say, "I will, be thou clean," and the work will be done. You will not get a Pure Heart from your fellow-creatures; if ever the treasure is yours, you will get it from God, and you will get it by Faith.

2. Purification will not be effected by any ceremonials, meetings, kneeling at the mercy-seat, singing of songs, or the like, apart from the Spirit of God. These forms and observances can wonderfully help you. Oh, what a marvelous influence goes out from soul to soul, when Comrades kneel together, and join heart and hand to seek God's sanctifying grace! But such gatherings will be a curse, rather than a blessing, unless they carry you on to that simple Faith in God Himself which claims and receives the sanctifying power.

3. Purification of the heart my Comrades, is not by knowledge. It is true, you must know something about the treasure you seek. For instance, you must know what Purity means; that it is possible to you, and that God will give it to you when you trust Him for it. But you may know all this, and a thousand times more, and be no nearer its realization, if that is all. The Israelites knew that Canaan was just over Jordan. They were quite sure of it. They could see the hills and dales of the country they had sought so long; but they were not in possession of the land, and died without ever setting their weary feet in it.

What a number of my dear Soldiers love to read, and hear, and talk, and sing about Holiness. They are never tired of the subject. They know all about it, but stop short of the Faith which alone can bring them into its enjoyment.

4. The Purifying of the heart is not by repentance. Some people are always mourning over the sins of their hearts and the inconsistencies of their lives. Oh, how they hate their coldness and

pride, and worldliness and bad temper, and the other evil things that still cling to their heart and make them trouble. Oh, how ashamed they are of the feebleness of their love for Christ, the littleness of their zeal for His Kingdom, and the lukewarmness of their concern for souls. They are constantly giving up their evil ways and promising to do better. But this repenting and renouncing does not help them, because they do not go on to that definite act of Faith that brings deliverance from the evils over which they mourn.

5. The Purification of your hearts, my Comrades, will not come by your personal consecration to the service of God, if you simply stop there. What you want is, not only the readiness to do the Will of God, but the Power to do it.

This Purification is, as the Apostle says, "by Faith." It is by Faith that the soul presses on beyond desire and knowledge, and repentance and consecration, and says, "The blessing is mine." This is the last round in the Salvation Ladder. You may have to climb up by all, or only some of the steps I have named; but you must reach this step, or you cannot enter the Temple of Holiness. You say "I desire," "I repent," "I consecrate." Good, very good, excellent; but can you, will you, not take the last step, and say "I believe that He purifies me now"?

Yours affectionately,

William Booth

"Answer that gracious end in me
For which Thy precious life was given,
Redeem from all iniquity,
Restore, and make me meet for heaven;
Unless Thou purge my every stain,
Thy suffering and my faith are vain.

"Didst Thou not in the flesh appear
Sin to condemn, and man to save?
That perfect love might cast out fear?
That I Thy mind in me might have?
In Holiness show forth Thy praise,
And serve Thee all my spotless days?

"Didst Thou not die that I might live
No longer to myself, but Thee?
Might body, soul, and spirit give
To Him who gave Himself for me?
Come then, my Master, and my God,
Take the dear purchase of Thy Blood."

Chapter 8: Purifying Faith

That Christ may dwell in your hearts by faith; that ye, being rooted and grounded in love, may be able to comprehend with all saints what is the breadth, and length, and depth, and height, and to know the love of Christ, which passeth knowledge, that ye might be filled with all the fullness of God.
- Ephesians 3:17-19 -

My Dear Comrades,

You will remember that when I closed my last Letter, I was considering a very interesting part of our subject; namely, that particular act of Faith which purifies the heart. I said something to you then on this question; but I must have another word, because I fancy that it is here that many of my dear people stumble and fail in seeking the Blessing of Purity. They come to the door of full deliverance from Sin; they look inside the Temple of Holiness; they long to be there; but they hesitate to take the step which alone can carry them in.

They cannot, or do not, or will not exercise the Faith that purifies, and so turn away and go back to the unsatisfactory state of sinning and repenting in which they have lived so long. Now, I feel quite sure that this is often caused by ignorance or mistaken notions; and I would, therefore, very much like to explain a little further what that wonderful Faith is by which the soul enters into the enjoyment of a Full Salvation.

I may have again to pass over some of the ground we have already traveled together. But that cannot be helped. I had better repeat myself a thousand times and be understood, than leave you in doubt as to my meaning.

1. I remark that Purifying Faith is the Faith that has some definite knowledge of the nature of the Blessing desired, and the means by which it is attained. That knowledge may be very imperfect, but it is enough to apprehend the nature of the Purity sought for. This Faith sees that Purity is not merely a passing wave of feeling or a deliverance from temptation. It perceives that it is not a condition of uninterrupted happiness, but a state of Holiness in which the servant of God ceases to grieve the Holy Spirit, obeys the

call of duty, and loves Him with all the power he possesses.

Purifying Faith fixes its eye on the Blessing, and says "I want a Pure Heart, I need it; it is the Will of God that I should have it. Christ bought it for me when He died on the Cross. O God, let it be mine."

Has your Faith got as far as that, my Comrades? Do you see what Purity means? If so that is a gratifying attainment. Hold it fast until God bestows the great treasure upon you.

2. Purifying Faith sets the soul longing after the possession of this Treasure. Looking at a thing which you consider valuable and possible, will certainly awaken the desire for its possession. If I am informed of some site of land, or some piece of property, which I could see would be of great service to The Army, the more I think about it, the longer I look at it, the more strongly shall I desire its possession.

It is so with Holiness, my Comrades. If you believe it to be the precious thing it really is, you will consider it, keep it before your mind, turn it round and round, and the more you do so the more you will desire it. Does your Faith compel your attention? Does it make you think? "O Lord, increase our Faith." If you will only keep on looking at it you will come to long after it with earnest desire.

3. Purifying Faith is the Faith that leads the soul to choose the Blessing. It says, "I'll have it if it is for me," and sings:

"Give me the Faith that Jesus had,
The Faith that can great mountains move,
That makes the mournful spirit glad,
The saving Faith that works by Love;
The Faith for which the saints have striven,
The Faith that pulls the fire from Heaven."

Purifying Faith goes further than merely admiring and talking, and longing and praying: it elects to make the experience its own. It says, "Now, Lord, this great deliverance shall be mine. I choose it. If it is to be attained, I'll have it!" We all know how the sinners around us pain our hearts by the way they trifle with Salvation. They say, "Oh, yes, it is good, and it's very kind of Jesus Christ to make it possible for us to be saved. We must have Salvation. We must not be lost. But we won't seek it now." Even so, I am afraid many Soldiers trifle with holiness. They say, "I ought to be holy; I wish I were holy. O Lord, make me holy - but not now." But Purifying Faith chooses the Blessing desired. It says, "I'll begin to seek now with all my heart - and I'll seek until I find."

4. Purifying Faith compels the surrender of everything that stands in the way of the possession of Holiness. It is willing to pay the price. Oh, how cheerfully people give up pleasant things in order to gain those which they believe to be still more desirable. So here, when men really do see and believe in the worth of Purity, they will be ready to abandon everything which seems likely to hinder them obtaining it.

Oh, my Comrades, have you got thus far? Does your Faith duly value the treasure we are talking about? If not, it cannot be said to be Purifying Faith. If it does, it will cry out.

"Is there a thing beneath the sun,
That strives with Thee my heart to share?
Oh, tear it thence, and reign alone,
Then shall my heart from earth be free
When it has found repose in Thee."

5. Purifying Faith leads the soul to the consecration of all it possesses to the service of its Saviour.

Now, my dear Comrades, has your Faith got as far as this? I am afraid many come close up to this point, and then grow afraid. They shrink from the full consecration, and give up the holy strife. They will say, "If I place myself in the hands of God, for Him to do just as He likes with me, who can tell where He may send me, or what He may want me to do?"

For instance, I fancy some of my Soldiers hang back from the fear that God should say to them: You will have to put on the Uniform; or you will have to speak to your relatives about their souls; or you will have to plead with strangers; or you will have to be Officers, or do something else from which their unsanctified hearts turn back; and so they go no further in the search for Purity. But Purifying Faith sees Jesus Christ to be the altogether lovely, His service to be infinitely desirable, and the privilege of joining with Him in the work of saving and blessing men so honorable and desirable that the soul controlled by it leaps forward to lay itself at the Master's feet, willing to be used in any way He thinks best, and so gladly offers a consecration which knows no hesitation, has no reservation, the limits of which being only bounded by its ability.

6. But Purifying Faith goes further than this: it realizes that Holiness has been bought by the Sacrifice of Jesus Christ, and is promised in the unchanging word of God. Do you see that this Treasure of treasures is yours, my Comrades, and that God, having provided and promised it, is now waiting and willing to give it you?

Faith hears God say, "From all your filthiness, and from all your idols, will I cleanse you." Faith replies, "True, Lord, and I am waiting and longing for it to be done. It shall be mine."

Faith hears Him say, "I will take away the heart of stone - the hardness from your heart, and give you a heart of flesh - a tender heart," and answers.

"Lord, I am sure you will. I trust you to do it now. The hour of my sanctification is at hand, The Cleansing Spirit is coming to dwell within me. He will make and keep me clean."

7. But Purifying Faith goes further still. it believes that it actually receives the Purity which it seeks. It says not only "God is willing and waiting to save," but "Jesus does sanctify me now."

My Comrades, I want to ask you the question, When shall this Purity come into your hearts? Do you say tomorrow? I answer, "Perhaps it may be tomorrow. I do not know whether it may." Do you say, "When I am dying"? I answer, "Perhaps it may be when you are dying, but I do not know whether it will be possible then." Do you say NOW? I answer "YES, IT CAN BE NOW," for "Now is the accepted time, and Now is the day of Salvation."

Yours affectionately,

William Booth

Chapter 9: Witnesses

But ye shall receive power, after that the Holy Ghost is come upon you: and
ye shall be witnesses unto Me both in Jerusalem, and in all Judea, and in
Samaria, and unto the uttermost part of the earth.
- Acts 1:8 -

My Dear Comrades,

Have you grown tired of my subject? I hope not. From my youth until this very day the subject of Holiness has always had an unspeakable charm for me. To pray and hear, and sing and believe, and testify to the power of the Precious Blood to cleanse from sin, and fill with love, and keep from falling, has been among the most precious privileges of my life. The charm is as fresh to me today as ever. I trust you feel as I do.

A devout Saint of old sang in words that always thrill my soul when I hear them:

"I'll carve His passion in the bark;
And every wounded tree
Shall droop, and bear some sacred mark
That Jesus died for me.
And men shall wonder as they read,
Inscribed through all the grove,
How Heaven itself came down to bleed,
To win a mortal's love.

Is not that beautiful, my Comrades? Ought not we Salvationists to be anxious to sound out, by our lips and lives, to the sons and daughters of men, at every opportunity the glorious fact, that Jesus Christ died not only to save men and women from open and deliberate sin, but to purify unto Himself "a peculiar people," inwardly as well as outwardly clean.

Has He wrought this deliverance for you, my Comrades? Or are you deterred from seeking it by doubts as to His ability to effect this purification of the heart? Let me call a few witnesses, who will testify to its realization in their own experience. I am sure you will listen to what they have to say. I will begin with the Saints of the Bible. Hear them. To begin with we read that:

1. Enoch walked with God three hundred years. God Himself testifies that Enoch's ways were pleasing in His sight. What a blessed testimony. Who can question that Enoch had a Pure Heart?

2. Noah was a good man and perfect in his generation. So far as he had the light he lived up to it. He condemned the world and became "heir of the righteousness," that is the holiness "which is by faith." He had a Pure Heart.

3. The Lord Himself testified, that Job was a perfect and an upright man. He was perfect in love, and perfect in faith. He was able to look up even in the darkest hour, and say, "Though He slay me, yet will I trust in Him." He loved God with all his heart, and his neighbor as himself. He had a Pure Heart.

4. We have a most remarkable testimony to Abraham's Faith and Obedience. God told him, as He tells you, to "Walk before Him, and be perfect," and we have the most striking evidence of Abraham's obedience to God in the offering up of his son Isaac. Who can doubt that he had a Pure Heart?

5. Isaiah was a Holy man. We read that when the Prophet acknowledged his uncleanness in the Temple, God's angel touched his lips with a live coal of fire from off the altar, and testified that his iniquity was taken away and his sin was purged. Whereupon Isaiah rose up and consecrated himself there and then to go out as the messenger of God. He had a Pure Heart.

6. Zacharias and Elizabeth his wife, we are informed, were both righteous. They walked in all the commandments of the Lord blameless. Being delivered out of the hand of their enemies, they served God without fear, in holiness and righteousness all the days of their lives.

7. The Apostle John testified that he was made perfect in love. "God is love," he says; "he that dwelleth in love, dwelleth in God, and God in him. Herein is our love made perfect, that we may have boldness in the day of judgment; because as He is, so are we in this world."

8. Paul called his comrades to witness that his life was a Holy life. "Ye are witnesses," he says to the Thessalonians, "how holily, justly, and unblameably we behaved ourselves among you."

But let me call a few witnesses of modern times. I testify that they belong to the choicest spirits who have ever walked this earth. I start off with the saint, John Fletcher, a Clergyman. He says: "I will confess Him to all the world, and I declare unto you in the presence of the Holy Trinity that I am dead indeed unto sin; Christ is my Prophet, Priest, and King, my indwelling Holiness, my All in All!" Hear another witness:

"All at once, I felt that a Hand, not feeble, but Omnipotent, not in wrath, but in love, was laid upon my brow. It seemed to diffuse through me a holy, self-consuming energy. The deeps of God's love swallowed me up. All its waves and billows rolled over me."

Hear the testimony of one of the holiest and most useful men ever possessed by the British Church - a man whom I admire more than words can tell: "My soul was all wonder, love, and praise. It is now twenty-six years ago; I have walked in this liberty ever since. Glory be to God! I have been kept by His power. By faith I stand."

A host of other testimonies are before me. One more is all I can find room for. Hear him. He says:

"I was alone in the field one beautiful day in the early spring. The sky clear, the sun glorious, the happy birds, and all nature, quick and springing into life, were but the symbol of my heart's experience. It was a glorious day within and without. I can never forget that day. I shall never enjoy a happier until I walk the fields of Paradise. 'What is it that you want?' seemed to be asked me. 'I want victory over all sin,' was my answer. 'Have you not got it?' 'Yes,' I replied. 'What else do you want?' I answered, 'I want power to perform all the known will of God.' 'Do you not do this?' 'Well, then, have you not received the blessing you have asked for?' And never from that hour have I doubted for a moment the reality of that work."

Comrades, I have convinced you that there is no fatal necessity laid on you to sin, either in word, or thought, or deed. I have declared to you the unchanging faithfulness and power of your redeeming God. And now, what will you do? Your Lord is waiting to bring you into the land of Perfect Purity, of Perfect Love. I have shown you how you can enter in. Again I beseech you to rise, and go up to possess the good land, in God's own way; that is, by Faith. But, do it now, and if at first you do not succeed, do not give up the search; but persevere, and try, and try, and try again.

Yours affectionately,
William Booth

"Now rise, exulting rise, my soul,
Triumphant sing the Saviour's praise;
His name through earth and skies extol,
With all thy power through all thy days."

Chapter 10: How To Keep Pure

Blessed is the man that endureth temptation, for when he is tried, he shall receive the crown of life, which the Lord hath promised to them that love Him.
- James 1:12 -

My Dear Comrades,

After trying to show you the desirability of this experience, and urging it upon your acceptance, I cannot help feeling that a few counsels bearing upon the best method of retaining the blessing of Holiness after it has been gained may be useful.

Beyond question many do find this sacred treasure of a Pure Heart, and exult in the confidence and joy it brings, who after a short season lose it again. They enter the Holy Temple, and then for one reason or another desert it. They struggle with tears and prayers up on to the Highway of Holiness, and then turn aside on to some by path or other, where they become the prey once more of the doubts and fears and sins of the olden time. This is a great pity. Those who act thus are the chief sufferers; but, alas! a great injury is also inflicted upon others by their unfaithfulness.

But the failure of those who obtain the grace to keep what they have received, should be no discouragement to you who have entered upon this holy path, and no argument against your persevering in it.

What you have to do, my Comrades, is to make up your minds, that having found the Pearl of Great Price no enemy shall rob you of the treasure. To this end my first counsel is:

1. Seek till you obtain a settled conviction in your own heart that the work is done. Be content with nothing less than the assurance that God has really and truly cleansed your soul from sin. Do not allow yourselves to rest in any pleasant feelings merely, or in any hope of a future revelation on the subject. Continue to wrestle, and pray, and believe, until you are satisfied that the work is accomplished. But do you ask again, "How can I tell whether God has cleansed my soul from sin?" I reply, "How did you find out that God had forgiven your sins? How did you come to know that precious fact?" for, assuredly, a precious fact it was when you were

48

saved. I suppose that since that gracious gift was yours, you have sung over, a thousand times or more, the words:

"I never shall forget the day
When Jesus washed my sins away."

"How did you come to the personal assurance that you were saved?" I ask, and you reply that God spoke it to your heart. Well, the assurance of your Sanctification will come in the same way. The Holy Spirit will produce a delightful persuasion in your soul that all the pride and malice, and envy and selfishness, have been taken away, and that God has filled you with peace and love.

This precious persuasion will, no doubt, come in different forms to different individuals. To some it will appear as the "Rest of Faith," to others as the "Baptism of Fire," to others as the "Fullness of Love," and to others as the "Enthronement of Christ" come to reign in their souls supreme over an inward Kingdom, which is righteousness, peace, and joy in the Holy Ghost. But to all alike when the work is real and complete there will be the conviction that the blood cleanses and that the heart is pure. Be content with nothing less than this, and leave to God's good pleasure the giving or the withholding of more.

2. Being satisfied that God has purified your heart confess the fact. You must do so, if you want to retain the Blessing. Many of the Holiest men and women the world has known have, under the influence of false modesty or diffidence or other motives, been hindered from avowing the wonderful things that God has done for them, and have thereby grieved the Holy Spirit and lost the Blessing. Satan will tempt you to hide your light under a bushel after the same manner, but you must resist him, and boldly confess to all around you the Salvation God has given you. Acknowledge it to yourselves. Say over and over again to your own heart:

"Glory, Glory, Jesus saves me;
Glory, Glory to the Lamb";
Now the Cleansing Blood has reached me,
Glory, Glory to the Lamb!"

Acknowledge it to your Saviour. Tell Him that you trust Him, and glorify Him for what He has done for you. Confess it to your Comrades at every reasonable opportunity. Let it be known in your own family. It may not only greatly help you, for those nearest and dearest to you to know what God has done for you, but it may prove a great blessing to them.

49

Of course you will be careful not to exhibit anything like a boastful spirit, and to give all the glory to God for all that He has given you to enjoy, and I am sure you will not make any professions as though you condemned those Comrades who have not been brought to see and possess this great Salvation. Love will be in all your words as well as in your heart.

But you must confess the fact that God has cleansed your heart, and that, by His Spirit, He enables you to live day by day without grieving Him. It may be, at times it will be, a cross. But you must take it up, and in doing so you will become a light and a power and a joy to your Comrades and friends.

3. To retain the Blessing you must strive to live in the same spirit of submission, obedience, and consecration to God as that which you entered into its enjoyment. Your everyday experience must be that which we often sing:

"Here then to Thee Thy own I leave,
Mold as Thou wilt Thy passive clay,
But let me all Thy stamp receive
And let me all Thy words obey,
Serve with a single heart and eye,
And to Thy glory live and die."

4. To keep this experience you must continue in the same spirit of trust that first brought the Blessing into your heart. You did not receive the gift of Purity by feelings or by knowledge or by works; no, nor by desire nor by prayer. You believed and you were saved. If you had said I won't, or I can't believe that Jesus cleanses, unless I feel the work to be done in my heart, you could not have rejoiced in its possession. You trusted and the work was done. You must go forward in that spirit. There will be hours when all will seem to be hard and dark and desolate. Those will be hours when you will have to fight the fight of faith, and to cling to the beginning of your confidence, whether you feel pleasant or unpleasant, whether your heart seems hard or tender, that the Blood cleanses. Hold it fast.

5. To keep a clean heart you must resist temptation. You will have temptation, it will come from different sources, but especially from the devil, in three particular directions:

(a) He will try to draw you aside into old habits, either doubtful in their nature or positively evil. He will know your weak points. Set a double watch there.

(b) He will suggest his own evil wishes and desires, and then seek to persuade you that they are from your own heart. He will say, "How can you be sanctified and have such sinful thoughts as those?" Disown his foul productions. Tell him they are not yours. Tell him that you hate them. Tell him they belong to him.

(c) He will strive to make you think you have lost the Blessing because you do not always feel as though you had it. But you are to live not by feeling but by faith.

6. To keep a pure heart you must carefully continue the use of such means as God has appointed for your assistance. Purity does not bring you into any state that renders the use of means for its maintenance and increase unnecessary.

7. To keep the Blessing:

(a) You must pray; and I strongly urge you to pray at stated hours, and for given periods. (b) You must read and study your Bible. (c) Read such books and papers as are instructive and encouraging on the subject of Holiness. (d) Watch as well as pray. Be ever on your guard.

8. Keep on fighting for souls, do not be led off into a selfish occupation with your own experience, or in promoting the same experience in other Comrades. I think it is right and proper that you should devote a portion of your time and energy to the duty of sanctifying yourselves and of spreading a full Salvation among your Comrades. But nothing can relieve you from the duty of fighting for the Salvation of dying souls around you.

I have only space for one other word. It is one of deep importance. With all the emphasis I can command I would say to every reader of these Letters, if from any cause whatever you should lose the assurance that the blood of Jesus cleanses you; or if, more melancholy still, you should lose the blessing of Purity, fly at once to your Saviour's feet, confess your wrongdoing, give yourself up again to the full service of your Lord, and once more plunge in the Fountain opened for sin and uncleanness; and then, profiting by the sorrow and disappointment of your fall, start afresh to live the life of faith in a purifying Saviour.

Yours affectionately,

William Booth

"What though a thousand hosts engage
A thousand worlds my soul to shake,
I have a shield shall quell their rage,
And drive the alien armies back:
Portrayed it bears a bleeding Lamb,
I dare believe in Jesus' name.

"Me to retrieve from Satan's hands,
Me from this evil world to free,
To purge my sins and loose my bands,
And save from all iniquity,
My Lord and God from heaven He came;
I dare believe in Jesus' name."

END

For hundreds of other excellent titles see:

www.**Classic***Christian***Ebooks**.com

THE SEVEN SPIRITS

Or

What I Teach My Officers

By
General William Booth

THE SEVEN SPIRITS

TABLE OF CONTENTS

Prefatory Note.

This volume contains the outlines of a series of Addresses by General Booth, delivered to Salvation Army Officers at the International Congress held in London, in June, 1904. That which is here printed does not profess to be a verbatim report of those Addresses, but is merely a reproduction of the written notes from which The General spoke, and is issued in this form in reply to an oft-repeated request for information as to the teaching given by The General to his Officers.

International Headquarters,

May 1907.

Chapter 1: Introduction

Section I.

I. A great opportunity lies before The Army, and before you as representatives of The Army. You have looked at that opportunity; you have wondered about it, and, if you are men and women of God, which I believe you are, your souls are stirred with gratitude at the thought that God has honoured you by any association with a movement that has been the means of so greatly glorifying Him, and so largely blessing the world.

II. The use that is made of this mighty opportunity for promoting the happiness of mankind, and the glory of the God of Heaven, very largely depends upon the Field Officers of The Salvation Army. Officers make the character of the armies they lead. This is true of military armies—Napoleon not only led his army, but made it. This is true of commercial armies. The great financiers and traders mould the business world. The same may be said of political armies. This is equally true, if not more so, of Salvation Armies. On you, then, this responsibility rests. The Field Officer especially fashions the force he controls, chiefly in three ways: by his mind, character, and methods. In short, he constitutes the mould in which those whom he commands will be cast. The shape you give the men and women under your command today will go down to the third, the fourth, and the fifth generations. You are making the kind of Salvationists who will be walking about here five hundred years hence, if the world lasts so long.

If the Officer is a coward, those whom he commands will be cowards. If he is holy, they will be holy. If he is a man of resistless courage and daring, they will be like him. Our responsibility for success or failure is therefore enormous. Where we are successful we are not only gaining victories today, but making the conquerors of the future. Let us remember—we shall have to give an account of our stewardship; we are passing over, one by one, to that great Tribunal. My dear wife, Commissioner Dowdle, the Consul, have all gone to give their account. We too shall have to go. The words,

"Behold I come quickly," are ever sounding in my ears.

III. What kind of Officers are required to meet this opportunity? I think I possess some ability for pointing out the qualities needed for satisfactorily answering this question.

1. I have read my Bible and pondered over the great responsibilities which lie at the very foundation of an Officer's duties. I hope I have not read that Book in vain.

2. I have listened to the voice of the Spirit of God within me. He has shown me something of what an Officer should be and do, in order that he may efficiently fulfil the mission to which he has been called.

3. I have studied the hearts and circumstances of the men you are sent to save. Human nature is, as we very often say, much the same in all ages and in all places. What I have seen of the failings, the prejudices, and the sins of men with regard to religion during my life should be of service in helping and guiding you in your warfare.

4. I have profited by the experience of other warriors on the field: from those of the prophets down to the last Army Captain who has any reputation for bringing men to God. In the days of old, men walked over land, and sailed over water, thousands of miles, penetrating the depths of barren wildernesses and tractless forests, in order to gaze upon some skeleton hermit who had acquired a special reputation for holiness, or who had gained a more intimate knowledge than his fellows of the dealings of God with men. Something like this has been my custom ever since I was a youth, fifteen years of age. To hear of anyone possessing any extra skill in soul-saving has been enough to excite my curiosity, lead me to seek a knowledge of their doings, and carry me to their feet. Surely, I must have learned something from these worthies. What I have learned I want to tell you.

5. I have studied the needs of the world around me. A large part of my life has been spent in considering and mourning over the sins and sorrows of men, and in making plans for their deliverance.

6. I have had some personal experience in this warfare. It is nearly sixty years now since I made my first attempt to influence men in favour of salvation. Could I tell the number of individuals whom during that time I have seen kneeling at the mercy-seat it would sound like a fiction. Perhaps I have been as highly privileged

in this respect as any man that ever lived. God has indeed endorsed my work with His blessing. I think I know you, my comrades, and have some idea of what you are able to do, and the circumstances in which you are called to labour, and I am sure my heart will not allow me to ask from you what is beyond your ability to give. Nothing can be gained by seeking impossibilities.

Section II.

I. I propose to tell you frankly what I think is the kind of Officer called for at this juncture of our history; and, among other things, I think he should answer to the following description:

1. He should be possessed of the Spirit of Divine Life. Dead things will be of no use here.

2. He should be possessed of the Spirit of Holiness. Sanctified men are the world's great need.

3. He should be possessed of the Spirit of Supreme Devotion to the Object of The Army. Given up without any secret reservations.

4. He should be possessed of the Spirit of Light. Making men know themselves, and know the things of God.

5. He should be possessed of the Spirit of War. With fighting Officers the Army can conquer the world.

6. He should be possessed of the Spirit of Faith. "All things are possible to him that believeth."

7. He should be possessed of the Spirit of Burning Love. Love never faileth. Love shall be the conqueror.

II. You may take the possession of these qualifications as being the will of God concerning every one of you. You may take them as commandments coming directly from God Himself. In the book of Revelation John speaks of the Seven Spirits of God which are before His Throne, and which go out into all the earth to make men know what is the mind of God respecting them. These Seven Spirits are still travelling to and fro on their heavenly mission. These Seven Spirits have voices, and speak to the consciences of men. They wait to speak to us. They proclaim what is their Master's will concerning the Officers of The Salvation Army. They will come to dwell with us, and help us to carry out the object for which we exist. Shall we hear them? Shall we receive them? What do you say? I know your mind. I answer for you. Yes, certainly we will. Let us welcome them as the messengers of God. This they most certainly are.

Section III.

I. Here they come. The first Spirit enters. Look at him. Oh, vision of beauty! How can I paint him? More beautiful in appearance, but in appearance only, than those who follow him. Lovely roses on his cheeks; quick, vigorous, and active his every movement, while his eyes flash every moment with lustrous light and living fire. In his hand he holds a banner. On one side it bears a representation of the morning sun, and on the other a white-robed spirit rising from the tomb. This is the Spirit of Life. He speaks. Listen! He says: "*O Officers, Officers, I am one of the Seven Spirits whom John saw. I travel up and down the earth on special errands of mercy. I am come from Him that sitteth on the Throne, and reigneth for ever and ever, to tell you that if you are to succeed in your life-and-death struggle for God and man, the first thing you must possess, in all its full and rich maturity, is the Spirit of Divine Life.*"

II. And now here is the second Spirit. Beautiful again, beautiful beyond human conception or description; benign of countenance, and calm and restful in manner, with gentle and heart-moving speech; clothed in white and spotless raiment; holy and undefiled. This is the *Spirit of Purity. But see, he spreads forth his wings and looks down upon us and speaks. Hear him:* "*O Officers, Officers, the Great Father has sent me to tell you that if you would be successful in your campaign against wickedness, selfishness, and fiends, you must yourselves be holy.*"

Ill. Now enters the third Spirit. Look at him. He is of an even more imposing appearance than those who have preceded him. Upon his shoulders is inscribed a crimson cross; round his loins is a girdle of blood-stained raiment. His bosom heaves with anguish on account of the oppressions, sins, and miseries of a suffering world. This is the Spirit of Devotion. Hear him. He speaks: "*O Officers, Officers, you must be supremely given up to the saving of men.*"

IV. And now here comes the fourth Spirit. Look at him. He has a strong, determined countenance, and there is a fiery Cross upon his breast. In his right hand he holds a flaming sword, and in his left a summons to the judgment Bar. This is the Spirit of War. Now he speaks. Hear him: "*O Officers, Officers, you must fight devils, lies, fleshly indulgences, hardships, disappointments, and everything that sets itself up*

62

against God, or that is opposed to the living of a holy life, or which threatens the damnation of men. O Officers, at all risks and consequences you must fight for God and the salvation of souls."

V. Now enters the fifth Spirit. Here he comes, bright as the sun at noonday, with eyes before and behind, while shafts of living light go forth from his brow at every turn. See, he holds the Word of God in one hand, and the Morning Star in the other. This is the Spirit of Truth. Hear him. He speaks: "O Officers, Officers, your work is to make men know the unchanging and the unchangeable truth about the Love of God, the efficacy of the Blood of the Lamb, the accursedness of evil, the cruelty of the devil, the terrors of the Great White Throne, the joys of Heaven, and the horrors of the damnation of Hell. To do this you must be filled with the Light yourselves."

VI. Now for the sixth Spirit. Behold him - with eyes lifted up to Heaven and steadfastly fixed on the Throne of God; with bold, unshrinking confidence stamped on every feature. In his hand he holds a crimson banner, on which there is inscribed in letters of gold: "I believe." This is the Spirit of Faith. He speaks. Hear him: "O Officers, Officers, you cannot do without me. Listen to my words. If you treasure them up in your hearts, and carry them out in your lives, you shall be conquerors. If you neglect them, you will be defeated, no matter how brave you are in other things. You must take the inscription on my banner as your life-long motto. You must believe. You must do it night and day, in sorrow and joy, in defeat and in victory, living and dying. You must be men and women of Faith."

VII. But here comes the most beautiful and enhancing Spirit of all. Who can describe her? No one, for she is divine. Her countenance beams with holy affection, and speaks of inward rapture, and yet her eyes are full of compassionate tears. She is enveloped in a celestial flame, the emblem of the fire that is burning in her breast, while her arms are extended as though they would enfold the whole sinning, sorrowing world in their embrace. Oh, loveliest of all God's creations, who art thou? This is the Spirit of Burning Love. Hear her. She speaks: "O Officers, Officers; commissioned by the great 'I Am,' I come to tell you that in all you think, or speak, or do love must be the ruling passion of your lives. You must love each other. You must love your Soldiers. You must love poor sinners. You must love God; and that not after a fickle, cold, half-hearted fashion, but with a changeless, quenchless, burning love."

What shall we say to these Spirits? What reply shall they carry back to the Throne? What answer shall we give to the appeals they make to us in our own hearts? Let us say, "O ye Seven Spirits, we believe; nay, we feel that you have brought us the words of God Himself; and those words we will, more than ever, set ourselves to obey."

And in order that we may do so, my comrades, let us consider them in the order in which their messages have been given to us.

Chapter 2: The Spirit Of Life

Section I.

We begin with the good Spirit—the Spirit of Life. What did he say? What were the words he brought to us from the Throne? Let me repeat them: "*O Officers, Officers, I am one of the Seven Spirits whom John saw. I travel up and down the earth on special errands of mercy. I am come from Him that sitteth on the Throne, and reigneth for ever and ever, to tell you that if you are going to succeed in your life-and- death struggle for God and man, the first thing you must possess, in all its full and rich maturity, is the Spirit of Divine Life.*"

I. Now, before I go to the direct consideration of this message, let me have a word or two about life itself. Life, as you know, is the opposite principle to death. To be alive is to possess an inward force capable of action without any outside assistance. For instance: anything that has in it the principle by which it is able to act in some way, independent of the will of any other thing or creature outside of itself, may be said to be alive. It has in it the principle of life.

II. This principle of life is the mainspring and glory of God's Universe. We have it in different forms in this world. For instance:

1. We have material life. There is living and dead water, and there is living and dead earth.

2. Then there is vegetable life. In the fields, and woods, and gardens, you have living trees, and flowers, and seeds.

3. Then there is animal life. Only think of the variety, and usefulness, and instinctive skill of unnumbered members of the animal world.

4. Then, rising higher in the scale of being, you have human life. Every man, woman, and child possesses, as it were, a trinity of existence; namely, physical life, mental life, and soul life; each being a marvel in itself.

5. Then, rising higher still, we have a life more important, and

bringing more glory to God than any of the other forms that I have noticed, and that is Spiritual Life.

SECTION ll.

On this Spiritual Life let me make one or two remarks.

I. Spiritual Life is Divine in its origin. It is a creation of the Holy Spirit. I need not dwell on this truth. Jesus Christ was at great trouble to teach it. "Marvel not," He said, "ye must be born again. That which is born of the flesh is flesh, and that which is born of the Spirit is spirit." You have gone through this experience yourselves. You must insist on it in your people. Spiritual life proceeds from God. It can be obtained in no other way.

II. Spiritual Life not only proceeds from God, but partakes of the Nature of God. We see this principle, that the life imparted partakes of the nature of the author of being that imparts it, illustrated around us in every direction. The tree partakes of the nature of the tree from which it is derived. The animal partakes of the nature of the creature that begets it. The child partakes of the nature of its parents. So the soul, born of God, will possess the nature of its Author. Its life will be divine.

This is a mystery. We cannot understand it, but the Apostle distinctly affirms it when he says, the Son of God is a partaker of the Divine nature.

III. Spiritual Life, like all other life, carries with it the particular powers belonging to its own nature. Every kind of life has its own particular powers — senses, instincts, or whatever they may be called:

1. Vegetable life has its powers, enabling it to draw nutrition out of the ground.

2. Fish life has power adapting it to an existence in the water.

3. Animal life has powers or senses suitable to its sphere of existence, such as: seeing, hearing, tasting, and the like.

4. Human life has: (a) Faculties, emotions, loves and hatreds, suitable to its manner of existence. (b) And it has its own peculiar destiny. It goes back to God, to be judged as to its conduct when its earthly career terminates. (c) And the spiritual life of which we are speaking has powers or faculties necessary to the maintenance of its existence,

and to the discharge of the duties appropriate to the sphere in which it moves. For instance: it has powers to draw from God the nourishment it requires; it has powers to see or discern spiritual things; it has powers to distinguish holy people; it has powers to love truth, and to hate falsehood; it has powers to suffer and sacrifice for the good of others. It has powers to know, and love, and glorify its Maker.

IV. Those possessed of this Spiritual Life, like all other beings, act according to their nature. For instance: the tree grows in the woods, and bears leaves and fruit after its own nature. The bird flies in the air, builds its nest, and sings its song after its own nature. The wild beasts roam through the forest, and rage and devour according to their own nature. If you are to make these or any other creatures act differently, you must give them a different nature. By distorting the tree, or training the animal, or clipping the wings of the bird, you may make some trifling and temporary alteration in the condition or conduct of these creatures; but when you have done this, left to themselves, they will soon revert to their original nature.

By way of illustration. A menagerie recently paid a visit to a northern town. Amongst the exhibits was a cage labelled "The Happy Family," containing a lion, a tiger, a wolf and a lamb. When the keeper was asked confidentially how long a time these animals had lived thus peacefully together, he answered, "About ten months. But," said he, with a twinkle in his eye, "the lamb has to be renewed occasionally." As with these forms of life, so with men and women and children. The only way to secure conduct of a lasting character different from its nature is by effecting a change in that nature. Make them new creatures in Christ Jesus and you will have a Christlike life.

V. The presence of the powers natural to Spiritual Life constitutes the only true and sufficient evidence of its possession. The absence of these powers shows conclusively the absence of the life. If a man does not love God and walk humbly with Him; if he does not long after holiness, love his comrades, and care for souls, it will be satisfying evidence that he has gone back to the old nature — that is, to spiritual death.

VI. All Spiritual Life is not only imparted by Jesus Christ, but sustained by direct union with Him. "I am the Vine," He says, "ye are the branches; he that abideth in Me, and I in him, bringeth forth much fruit; for without Me ye can do nothing." (John 15:6.)

VII. Nothing will make up for the lack of this life. This, indeed, applies to every kind of existence.

1. You cannot find a substitute for life in the vegetable kingdom. Try the trees in the garden. Look at that dead apple tree. As you see it there, it is useless, ugly, fruitless. What will make up for the absence of life? Will the digging, or the manuring of the ground around it do this? No! That will be all in vain. If it is dead, there is only one remedy, and that is to give it life — new life.

2. Take the animal world. What can you do to make up for the lack of life in a dog? I read the other day of a lady who had a pet dog. She loved it to distraction. It died. Whatever could she do with it to make up for its loss of life? Well, she might have preserved it, stuffed it, jewelled its eyes, and painted its skin. But had she done so, these things would have been a disappointing substitute. So she buried it, and committed suicide in her grief, and was buried by its side.

3. Take the loss of human life. What is the use of a dead man? Go to the death-chamber. Look at that corpse. The loved ones are distracted. What can they do? They may dress it, adorn it, appeal to it. But all that human skill and effort can conceive will be in vain. All that the broken hearts can say or do must soon terminate, as did Abraham's mourning for Sarah, when he said, "Give me a piece of land that I may bury my dead out of my sight." Nothing can make up for the lack of life.

4. But this is specially true of the spiritual life of which we are speaking. (a) Take this in its application to a Corps. If you want an active, generous, fighting, dare-devil Corps, able and willing to drive hell before it, that Corps must be possessed, and that fully, by this spirit of life. Nothing else can effectively take its place. No education, learning, Bible knowledge, theology, social amusements, or anything of the kind will be a satisfactory substitute. The Corps that seeks to put any of these things in the place of life will find them a mockery, a delusion, and a snare; will find them to be only the wraps and trappings of death itself. (b) And if it is so in the Corps, it is so ten thousand times more in the Officer who commands that Corps — in you!

Section III.

I. Spiritual Life is the essential root of every other qualification required by a Salvation Army Officer.

1. With it he will be of unspeakable interest. (a) He will be a pleasure to himself. There is an unspeakable joy in having healthy, exuberant life. (b) He will be of interest to those about him. Who cares about dead things? Dead flowers—throw them out. Dead animals-eat them. Dead men-bury them. Dead and dying Officers— take them away. Give them another Corps. If he is living he will be of interest to all about him. Men with humble abilities, if full of this spiritual life, will be a charm and a blessing wherever they go. Look at the lives and writings of such humble men as Billy Bray, Carvosso, and Hodgson Casson. Their memory is an ointment poured forth today after long years have passed away.

2. Without this life an Officer will be of no manner of use.

No matter how he may be educated or talented, without life is to be without love; and to be without love, the Apostle tells us, is to be only as "a sounding brass." But it is not that of which I want to speak just now.

II. Spiritual Life is essential to the preservation of life. The first thing life does for its possessor is to lead him to look after its own protection.

1. When the principle of life is strong, you will have health and longevity.

2. When it is weak, you have disease.

3. When it is extinct, you have decay and rottenness.

III. Only vigorous Spiritual Life will enable a Salvation Army Officer to effectually discharge the duties connected with his position. Life is favourable to activity. It is so with all life. Go into the tropical forests, and see the exuberant growth of everything there. Look at the foliage, the blossom, the fruit. Look at the reptiles crawling at your feet, and take care they do not sting you. Look at the birds chattering and fluttering on the trees, and they will charm you. Look at the animals roving through the woods, and take care they do not devour you. Contrast all this movement with the empty, barren, silent, Polar regions or the dreary, treeless sands of the African desert. Go and look at the overflowing, tireless activity of the children. Why are they never still? It is the life that is in them. Go to the man at work. With what glee, and for what a trifling remuneration, he sweats, and lifts and carries the ponderous weights. Go to the soldier in the military war. How he shouts and sings as he marches to deprivations, and wounds, and death. Even so with spiritual life. It never rests; it never tires; it always sees something great to do, and is always ready to undertake it. What is the explanation? How can we account for it? The answer is, Life—abundant life.

IV. It is only by the possession of life that The Salvation Army Officer can spread this life. That is, reproduce himself, multiply himself, or his kind. This reproduction or multiplication of itself is a characteristic of all life.

1. Take the vegetable kingdom. Every living plant has life-producing seed, or some method of reproducing itself. The thistle: who can count the number of plants that one thistle can produce in a year? One hundred strawberry plants can be made in ten years to produce more than a thousand million other strawberry plants!

2. Take the animal kingdom. Here each living creature has this reproductive power. They say that a pair of sparrows would in ten years, if all their progeny could be preserved, produce as many birds as there are people on the earth-that is, 1,500,000,000. "Ye are of more value than many sparrows."

3. Just so, this spiritual life is intended to spread itself through the world.

It is to this end it is given to you. God's command to Adam was, "Be fruitful, and multiply, and replenish the earth." How much more does this command apply to you and to me! You are to be progenitors of a world of men and women possessed of spiritual life; the parents of a race of angels. How this is to be done is another question. About that I shall have something to say as we go along. For the moment, I am simply occupied with the fact that you have to call this world of holy beings into existence by spreading this life. Every Officer here is located in a world of death. Sometimes we style it a dying world, and so it is on its human side, but on its spiritual side it is past dying; it is dead. By that I do not mean that the spiritual nature, that is the soul, ever ceases to be in any man. That will never come to pass. Perhaps nothing once created will ever cease to be. Anyway, man is immortal. The soul can never die. Neither do I mean that there is no spiritual life.

4. By spiritual death we mean that the soul is: (a) Separated from God; no union with Him. In a blind man the organ may be perfect, but not connected. (b) Inactive. No love for the things God loves. No hatred for the things He hates. Dead to His interests, His kingdom; dead to Him. (c) Corrupt, bad, devilish, etc.

What a valley of dry bones the world appears to the man whose eyes have been opened to see the truth of things. Verily, verily, it is one great cemetery crowded with men, women, and children dead in trespasses and sin. Look for a moment at this graveyard, in which the men around you may be said to lie with their hearts all dead and cold to Christ, and all that concerns their Salvation. Look at it. The men and women and children in your town are buried there. The men and women in your city, in your street. Nay, the very people who come to your Hall to hear you talk on a Sunday night are there. There they lie. Let us read the inscriptions on some of their tombs.

(i.) Here lies Tom Jones.

He had a beautiful nature, and a young virtuous wife, and some beautiful children. All starved and wretched through their father's selfish ways. He can't help himself. He says so. He has proved it. He is dead in drunkenness.

(ii.) Here lies Harry Please-Yourself.

Mad on footballing, theatres, music halls, dances, and the like. Nothing else morning, noon, or night seems to interest him. There he is, dead in pleasure.

(iii.) Here lies James Haughtiness.

Full of high notions about his abilities, or his knowledge, or his family, or his house, or his fortune, or his business, or his dogs, or something. There he is, dead in pride.

(iv.) Here lies Jane Featherhead.

Absorbed in her hats, and gowns, and ribbons, and companions, and attainments. There she is, dead in vanity.

(v.) Here lies Miser Graspall.

Taken up with his money — sovereigns, dollars, francs, kroner, much or little. "Let me have more and more" is his dream, and his cry, and his aim, by night and day. There he is, dead in covetousness.

(vi.) Here lies Sceptical Doubtall.

Hunting through the world of nature, and revolution, and providence, and specially through the dirty world of his own dark little heart, for arguments against God and Christ and Heaven. There he is, dead in unbelief.

(vii.) Here lies Jeremiah Make-Believe.

With his Bible Class and Singing Choir, and Sunday religion, and heartless indifference to the Salvation or damnation of the perishing crowds at his door. There he is, dead in formality.

(viii.) Here lies Surly Badblood.

Packed full of suspicions and utter disregards for the happiness and feelings of his wife, family, neighbours, or friends. There he is, dead in bad tempers.

(ix.) Here lies Dives Enjoy-Yourself.

Look at his marble tomb, and golden coffin, and embroidered shroud, and ermine robes. This is a man whose every earthly want is supplied — Carriages, music, friends. There he is, dead in luxury.

(x.) Here lies Dick Never-Fear.

His mouth is filled with laughter, and his heart with contempt when you speak to him about his soul. He has no anxiety, not he. He'll come off all right, never fear. Is not God merciful? And did not Christ die? And did not his mother pray? Don't be alarmed, God won't hurt him. There he is, dead in presumption.

(xi.) Here lies Judas Renegade.

His grave has a desolate look. The thorns and thistles grow over it. The occupant has money and worldly friends, and many other things, but altogether he gets no satisfaction out of them; he is uneasy all the time. There he is, dead in apostasy.

There are any number of other graves. It is interesting, although painful, to wander amongst them. All, or nearly all, their occupants are held down by a heavy weight of ignorance, a sense of utter helplessness. And all are bound hand and foot with chains of lust, or passion, or procrastination, of their own forging. In the midst of these graves you live, and move, and have your being.

What is your duty here? Oh, that you realised your true business in this region of death! Having eyes, oh! that you could see. Having ears, oh! that you could hear. Having hearts, oh! that you could feel. What are you going to do with this graveyard? Walk about it in heartless unconcern, or with no higher feeling than gratitude for having been made alive yourselves? Or will you content yourselves with strolling through it, taxing its poor occupants for your living while leaving them quietly in their tombs as hopeless as you found them? Heaven forbid! Well, then, what do you propose? What will you do?

Look after their bodies, and feed and nourish them, making the graveyard as comfortable a resting-place as you can? That is good, so far as it goes, but that is not very far. Will that content you? Decorate their graves with flowers and evergreens, and wreaths of pleasant things? Will that content you? Amuse them with your music, or the singing of your songs, or the letting off of your oratorical fireworks among their rotting corpses? Will that content you? Instruct them in doctrines and rescues and salvations in which they have no share? Will that content you?

No! No! No! A thousand times no! You won't be content with all that. God has sent you into this dark valley for nothing less than to raise these doom-struck creatures from the dead. That is your mission. To stop short of this will be a disastrous and everlasting calamity.

What do you say? It cannot be done? That is false. God would never have set you an impossible task. You cannot do it? That is false again. For you have done it before, again and again. There is not an Officer here who has not called some souls from the dead. Not one. How many thousands—how many tens of thousands, in the aggregate, have the Officers present at this Congress raised from the graves of iniquity? Who can tell? Go and do it again. Go and look at them. Go and have compassion on them. Go and represent Jesus Christ to them. Go and prophesy to them. Go and believe for them. And then shall bone come to bone, and there shall be a great noise, and a great Army shall stand up to live, and fight, and die for the living God.

Chapter 3: The Spirit Of Purity.

Section I.

And now we come to the consideration of the message of the second Spirit. Let us recall his words: "*O Officers, Officers, the Great Father has sent me to tell you that if you would be successful in your campaign against wickedness, selfishness, and fiends, you must yourselves be holy.*"

I come now to the task of showing, as far as I am able, what the plan of life is which God has formed for a Salvation Army Officer. What must an Officer be and do who wants satisfactorily to fill up the plan God has formed for him? Of course, there will in some respects be certain striking differences in that plan. But in the main there will be remarkable resemblances. The first thing that God asks is, that the Officer shall possess the character He approves. You might say the character that He admires. The very essence of that character is expressed in one word-Holiness.

In the list or qualifications for effective leadership in this warfare, The Salvation Army has ever placed Holiness in the first rank. The Army has said, and says today, that no other qualities or abilities can take its place. No learning, or knowledge, or talking, or singing, or scheming, or any other gift will make up for the absence of this. You must be good if you are to be a successful Officer in The Salvation Army.

1. Let us suppose that a comrade was to present himself before us this morning, and say, "I am a Salvationist. I want to be an Officer amongst you, and I want to be an Officer after God's own heart; but I am ignorant of the qualifications needed." If I were to ask you what I should say to this brother, I know what your answer would be. You would say, with one voice, "Tell him that, before all else, he must be a holy man."

2. Suppose, further, that I appeared before you myself for the first time at this Congress, and were to say to you: "My comrades, I have come to be your Leader. What is the first, the foundation,

quality I require for your leadership?" I know the answer you would give me. You would say, "O General, you must be a holy man."

3. If there were gathered before me, in some mighty building, the choicest spirits now fighting in The Salvation Army the world over — Commissioners and Staff Officers, Field Officers and Local Officers, together with Soldiers of every grade and class; and suppose, further, that standing out before that crowd, I was to propose the question: "In what position in our qualifications shall I place the blessing of Holiness?" you know what the answer would be. With a voice that would be heard among the multitudes in Heaven the crowd would answer: "Holiness must be in the first rank."

4. If this morning I had the privilege of ascending to the Celestial City, and asking the assembled angels in that mighty temple where, day and night, they worship the Great Jehovah: "What position ought Holiness to occupy in the qualifications needed by Salvation Army Officers in their fight on earth?" you know that angels and archangels, cherubim and seraphim, would join with the Seven Spirits that are before the Throne with one united shout, loud enough to make the ears of Gabriel tingle, and would answer, "Place it first."

5. If I could have the still greater privilege of kneeling before the intercessory Throne of my dear, my precious, my glorified Saviour, and of asking Him what position this truth should hold in the hearts and efforts of Salvation Army Officers, you know that He would answer: "Blessed are the pure in heart." Holiness comes first.

6. If, further still, borne on a burning seraph's wings I could rise to the Heaven of Heavens, and, like its holy inhabitants, be allowed to enter the holy of holies where Jehovah especially manifests His glory; and if, prostrate before that Throne, with all reverence I should ask the question: "What is the first and most important qualification a Salvation Army Officer must possess in order to do Your Blessed Will?" you have His answer already. You know that He would reply: "Be ye holy, for I am holy."

Section II.

What, then, is that Holiness which constitutes the first qualification of an Officer, and which is asked for by that blessed Spirit of Purity coming from the Throne of God? In replying to this question I cannot hope to do more than put you in remembrance of what you must already know.

I. **I will, however, to begin with, take the broad ground that Holiness, in the sense in which The Salvation Army uses the word, means entire deliverance from sin.** I shall explain myself as I go along. But I begin with the assertion that holy souls are saved from sin. You all know what sin is. And it is important that you should, and that you should be able to define it at a moment's notice to whomsoever may inquire. John says: "All unrighteousness is sin." That is, everything that a man sees to be actually wrong, that to him is sin. (a) Whether the wrong be an outward act, or an inward thought, or a secret purpose does not affect its character. If the act, or thought, or purpose is wrong to that particular soul it is sin. (b) Whether the wrong be done in public and blazoned abroad before the world as such, or whether it be committed in darkness and secrecy, where no human eye can follow it, matters not; it is sin. To be holy, I say, is to be delivered from the commission of sin. Is not that blessed?

II. **To be holy is to be delivered from the penalty of sin.** "The wages of sin is death." Holy men are fully and freely forgiven. One of the evidences of the possession of Holiness is the full assurance of that deliverance. Salvation from doubt as to this. Is not that blessed?

III. **Holiness includes deliverance from the guilt of sin.** Sin has a retributive power. At the moment of commission it implants a sting in the conscience, which, in the impenitent man, lights a flame, which, without the application of the Precious Blood, is never extinguished. In Holiness the sting is extracted, and the fire is quenched. Is not that blessed?

IV. **Holiness supposes deliverance from the defilement of sin.** Sin pollutes the imagination, defiles the memory, and is a filth-creating leaven, which, unless purged away, ultimately corrupts and rots the whole being. In Holiness all the filth is cleansed away. The soul is washed in the Blood of the Lamb. This is the reason for so much being said in the Bible, and in the experience of entirely sanctified people, about purity of heart. Is not that blessed?

V. **Holiness means complete deliverance from the bondage of sin.** Every time a sin is committed, the inclination to do the same again is encouraged, and those habits which belong to the evil nature are strengthened until they assume the mastery of the soul, and the soul comes more and more under the tyranny of evil. In conversion the chains that bind men to sin are broken, but the tendency to evil still lingers behind. In Holiness the bondage is not only entirely destroyed, and the soul completely delivered from these evil tendencies, but is free to do the will of God, so far as it is known, as really as it is done in Heaven. Is not that blessed?

VI. Holiness supposes the deliverance of the soul from the rule and reign of selfishness. The essence of sin is selfishness; that is, the unreasoning, improper love of self. The essence of Holiness is benevolence. Holy souls are mastered by love, filled with love. Is not that blessed?

Section III.

It will be seen, then, that the Officer who enjoys this experience of Holiness will have received power from God to live a life consciously separated from sin. A man cannot be living in a God-pleasing state if he is knowingly living in sin, or consenting to it, which amounts to the same thing. Let us look a little more closely at this.

I. Holiness will mean a present separation from all that is openly or secretly untrue. Anyone pretending to be doing the will of God, while acting untruthfully or deceitfully in his dealings with those around him, is not only guilty of falsehood, but of hypocrisy. To be holy is to be sincere.

II. Holiness means separation from all open and secret dishonesty. This applies to everything like defrauding another of that which is his just and lawful due.

III. Holiness also means separation from all that is unjust. Doing unto others as you would that they should do to you, may be truly described as one of the lovely flowers and fruits of purity.

IV. Holiness means salvation from all neglect of duty to God and man. All pretensions to Holiness are vain while the soul is living in the conscious neglect of duty.

1. A holy Officer will do his duty to his Maker. He will love God with all his heart—such a heart as he has, big or little. He will love and worship Him, and strive to please Him in all that he does.

2. A holy Officer will love his neighbour as himself. The law of love will govern his dealings with his family, comrades, neighbours-body and soul.

Section IV.

That is a beautiful experience which I am describing, is it not, my comrades? And you cannot be surprised that the Spirit of Purity should bring you the message that it is God's plan of life for you. Upon it let me make a few further remarks.

I. Holiness is a distinct definite state; a man can be in it or out of it.

II. Holiness is enjoyed partially or entirely by all converted people. It can be enjoyed partially. No one would say that every converted man was a holy man, and no one would say that every man who was not perfectly holy was not converted. But I should say, and so would you, that every truly converted man is the master of sin, although he may not be entirely delivered from it.

III. Then, again, Holiness is a continued growth in sincere souls. With faith, watchfulness, prayer, and obedience, the power of sin diminishes as the days pass along, and the strength of Holiness increases.

IV. The line which separates a state of entire from a state of partial Holiness may be approached very gradually, but there is a moment when it is crossed. The approach of death is often all but imperceptible, but there is a moment when the last breath is drawn. Just so there is a moment when the body of sin is destroyed, however gradual the process may have been by which that state has been reached. There is a moment when the soul becomes entirely holy-entirely God's.

V. By perseverance in the sanctified life spiritual manhood is reached, and the soul is perfected in love; that is maturity.

Section V.

Let me illustrate the doctrine of Holiness, in its varied aspects, by comparing its attainment to the ascent of a lofty mountain.

Come with me. Yonder is the sacred mount, towering far above the clouds and fogs of sin and selfishness. Around its base, stretching into the distance, as far as eye can reach, lies a flat, dismal, swampy country. The district is thickly populated by a people who, while professing the enjoyment of religion, are swallowed up in unreality about everything that appertains to salvation. They talk, and sing, and pray, and write, and read about it, but they are all more or less in doubt whether they have any individual part or lot in the matter. Sometimes they think they have a hope of Heaven, but more frequently they are afraid that their very hopes are a delusion. The land is haunted by troubling spirits continually coming and going, that point to past misdoings and coming penalties. Such venomous creatures as hatreds, revenges, lusts, and other evil passions are rife in every direction; while the demons of doubt and despair seem to come and go of their own free will, leading men and women on the one hand to indifference, worldliness, and infidelity, and on the other to darkness and despair. This wild dismal territory we will style "The Land of Uncertainty."

In the centre of this unlovable and undesirable country, the mountain of which I want to speak lifts its lofty head. Call it "Mount Pisgah" or "Mount Beulah," or, if you will, call it, "Mount Purity" - I like that term the best. But whatever you name it, there it is, rising up above the clouds and fogs of sin, and selfishness, and doubt, and fear, and condemnation that ever overhang the swampy land of Uncertainty, of which I have given you a glimpse. Look at it. There are some monster mountains in the natural world, but they are mere molehills alongside this giant height. Look at it again. Is it not an entrancing sight? Its lofty brow, crowned with a halo of glorious light, reaches far upwards towards the gates of endless day, those living on its summit having glorious glimpses of the towers and palaces of the Celestial City. The atmosphere is eminently promotive of vigorous health and lively spirits. But its chief claim is the purity of heart, the constant faith, the loving nature, and the consecrated self-sacrificing devotion of those who are privileged to dwell there. It must be a charming place. The multitudes whose feet have ever been permitted to tread its blessed heights think so. But while gazing on the entrancing sight, the question spontaneously arises: "How can I get there?" There is evidently no mountain railway nor elevator on which, while reclining on pillows of ease, and serenaded by music and song, you can be rapidly and smoothly lifted up to the blessed summit. Those who reach that heavenly height must climb what the Bible calls the "Highway of Holiness." And they will usually find it a rugged, difficult journey, often having to fight every inch of the way. But, once on the celestial summit, the travellers will feel amply repaid for every atom of trouble and toil involved in the ascent. The road to this glorious height passes through various plateau or stages which run all round the sides of the mountain, each different from the other, and each higher than the one that preceded it Travellers to the summit have to pass through each of these stages. Let me enumerate some of the chief among them.

I. To begin with, there is the awakening stage, where the climbers obtain their first fair view of this holy hill. It is here that the desire to make the ascent first breaks out. This longing is often awakened by reading various guide-books or holiness advertisements, such as The War Cry, or "Perfect Love," which set forth the blessedness experienced by those who make the heavenly ascent. Sometimes the desire to ascend the holy hill is awakened by the pure light which every now and then shines from the summit direct into the travellers' hearts. Or, it may be their souls are set on fire with a holy longing to be emptied of sin and filled with love by the burning testimonies of some of the people who live up there, but who come down into the valley every now and then to persuade their comrades to make the ascent. Anyway, it almost always happens when those who read these guide-books and listen to these testimonies begin to search their Bibles and cry to God for guidance, that a spirit of hunger and thirst sets in which gives them no rest until they themselves resolve to take the journey up the side of this wonderful mountain.

II. A little higher up, and you reach the starting stage. Here those who fully resolve upon seeking holiness of heart first enter their names in the "Travellers' Book." On this plateau I observe that there is a great deal of prayer. You can hear the earnest petitions going up to Heaven, whichever way you turn. And, much prayer as there is, you can hear much singing also. One of the favourite songs commences:

> *"O glorious hope of perfect love!*
> *It lifts me up to things above,*
> *It bears on eagles' wings;*
> *It gives my ravished soul a taste,*
> *And makes me for some moments feast*
> *With Jesus' priests and kings."*

There is another favourite song which begins:

> *"O joyful sound of Gospel grace!*
> *Christ shall in me appear;*

I, even I, shall see His face,
I shall be holy here."

III. But, still ascending, we come to the wrestling stage. Here the travellers are met by numerous enemies, who are in dead opposition to their ever reaching the summit. I observe that the enemies attack those travellers with doubts as to the possibility of ever reaching the mountain's top, and with scores of questions about apparently conflicting passages of Scripture, and contradictory experiences of Christian people; and, alas! with only too frequent success, for the whole plateau seems to be strewn with the records of broken resolutions relating to the renouncements of evil habits, tempting companions, and deluding indulgences. And I observe that lying about are many unfulfilled consecrations relating to friends, and money, and children, and time, and other things; in fact, this stage seems to be a strange mixture of faith and unbelief; so much so, that it is difficult to believe that we are on the slopes of Mount Purity at all. Here you will find posted on the sides of the rocks in all directions placards bearing the words: "The things I would do those I do not, and the things I would not do those I do, and there is no spiritual health in me." And up and down you will also see notice-boards warning would-be travellers not to climb any higher for fear they should fall again.

But, thank God, while many chicken-hearted souls lie down in despair on this plateau, or retrace their steps to the dreary regions below, others declare that there is no necessity for failure. These push forward in the upward ascent, singing as they go:

"Though earth and hell the word gainsay,
The word of God can never fail;
The Lamb shall take my sins away,
'Tis certain, though impossible;
The thing impossible shall be,
All things are possible to me."

IV. So, persevering with our journey, higher up, very much higher up, we come to the sin-mastering stage. This is a glorious plateau. All who enter it do so by the narrow passage of repentance towards God, and faith in our Lord Jesus Christ; receiving in their souls, as they pass the threshold, the delightful assurance or full and free forgiveness through the Blood of the Lamb. Here men and women walk with heads erect in holy confidence, and hearts glad with living faith, and mouths full of joyous song, and eyes steadily fixed on the holy light that streams from the summit of the mount above them. That holy beacon guide is ever calling on them to continue their journey, and ever directing them on the way. Those who have reached this stage have already made great and encouraging progress; for God has made them conquerors over their inward foes. The rule and reign of pride and malice, envy and lust, covetousness and sensuality, and every other evil thing have come to an end.

They triumph on that account, but the conflict is not yet ended. Sometimes the battling is very severe; but with patient, plodding faith they persevere in the ascent, singing as they go:

"Faith, mighty faith, the promise sees,
And looks to that alone;
Laughs at impossibilities,
And cries, 'It shall be done!' "

V. And now, close at hand, is the stage of deliverance, where the triumph is begun. And now, ten thousand Hallelujahs, let it be known to all the world around, that once on this plateau the separation from sin is entire; the heart is fully cleansed from evil; the promise is proved to be true, "They that hunger and thirst after righteousness are filled." At a great Christian Conference the other day an eminent divine said that The Salvation Army believed in a "perfect sinner," but that he believed in a "perfect Saviour." This, I contend, was a separation of what God has joined together, and which never ought to be put asunder. For, glory be to the Father, glory be to the Son, and glory be to the Holy Ghost, The Salvation Army believes, with its Lord, that a perfect Saviour can make a poor sinner into a perfect saint. That is, He can enable him to fulfil His own command, in which He says: "Be ye therefore perfect, even as your Father which is in Heaven is perfect." (Matthew 5:48.)

VI. But there is one plateau higher still which, like a tableland, covers the entire summit of the mountain, and that is the maturity stage. Here the graces of the Spirit have been perfected by experience, and faith, and obedience, and the soul does the will of God as it is done in Heaven, united in the eternal companionship of that lovely being — the Spirit of Purity.

What do you say to my holy mountain, my comrades? Are you living up there? Have you climbed as near to Heaven as that represents? If not, I want to make a declaration which you have often heard before, but which it will do you no harm to hear again;

namely, that it is the will of God that you should not only reach the very summit, but that you should abide there.

Section VI.

Do you ask why God wills that you should reach and abide on this holy mountain?

I. I reply it is the will of God that you and I, and every other Officer in this blessed Army, should be holy for His own satisfaction. God finds pleasure in holy men and holy women. We know what it is to find pleasure in kindred companions. It is to like to be near them. To want to live with them, or have them to live with us. It is to be willing to travel any distance, or put ourselves to any inconvenience to reach them. According to the Bible, that is just how God feels towards His faithful people. He finds satisfaction in their doings, and praying, and worship, and song. But when there is unfaithfulness or sin of any kind this pleasure is sadly marred, if not altogether destroyed. In such cases the pleasure is turned to pain, the satisfaction to loathing, and the love to hatred.

Hear what He says of Israel: "In all their affliction He was afflicted, and the angel of His presence saved them; in His love and in His pity He bare them, and carried them all the days of old." If for no other reason than the pleasure it will give to God, don't you think every Officer should, with all his might, seek for Holiness of heart and life?

II. Another reason why God wants you to live on that blessed mountain is the interest He feels in your welfare. He loves you. He has told you so again and again. He has proved His love by His deeds. Love compels the being entertaining the affection to seek the good of its object. He knows that sin is the enemy of your peace, and must mean misery here and hereafter. For this reason among others, He wants to deliver you from it. You will remember that by the lips of Peter God told the Jews that He had raised up His Son Jesus, and sent Him to bless them by turning every one of them away from his iniquities. That applies to you, my comrades.

You have heard it before; I tell it you again. Holiness is the royal road to peace, contentment, and joy for you. The love God bears you, therefore, makes Him ceaselessly long after your Holiness of heart and life. Will you not let Him have His way? Will you not do His will?

III. God wants every Officer to be holy, in order, that through

him He may be able to pour His Holy Spirit upon the people to whom that Officer ministers.

1. The men and women around you are in the dark. Oh, how ignorant they are of God and everlasting things! They cannot see the vile nature of the evil, and the foul character of the fiends that tempt and rule them. They do not see the black ruin that lies before them. So on they go, the blind leading the blind, till over the precipice they fall together. God wants their eyes to be opened. The Spirit can do the work, and through you He wants to pour the light.

2. The men and women around you are weak. They cannot stand up against their own perverted appetites, the charms of the world, or the devices of the devil. God wants to pour the Spirit of Power upon this helpless crowd. But He wants holy people through whom He can convey that strength. He works His miracles by clean people. That is His rule. There is nothing in the work of the early Apostles more wonderful than the miraculous manner in which they went about breathing the Spirit of Life and Light and Power on the people. But they were fully consecrated, Blood-and-Fire men and women. What do you say, my comrades? Will you be holy mediums? Do you not answer, "Thy will be done "?

IV. God wants you to be holy, in order that you may reveal Him to the world by your example. Men do not believe in God — that is, the real God — the God of the Bible; and they do not believe in Him, because they do not know Him. He seeks to reveal Himself to men in various ways.

1. He reveals Himself through the marvels of the natural world; and many say they can see God in the sun, and stars, and seas, and trees.

2. He reveals Himself by speaking to men in their own heart , and many hear His whisperings there.

3. He reveals Himself in His own Book, and some read and ascertain what is His mind there.

But, alas! the great multitude are like children. They require to see and hear God revealed before their very eye in visible and practical form before they will believe. And to reach these crowds, God wants men and women to walk about the world so that those around, believers and unbelievers alike, shall see the form and hear the voice of the living God; people who shall be so like Him in spirit, and life, and character as to make the crowds feel as though the very shadow of God had crossed their path. Will you be a shadow of

God?

V. God wants you to be holy, in order that you may know what His mind is about the world, and about your work in it.

1. He entertains certain opinions and feelings with respect to it. He has His own plan for saving it.

2. He wants to reveal to you what those opinions and feelings are, and to do this so far as it will be good for you and those about you. He wants you to know how you can best fight devils, convict sinners, save souls, and bless the world.

3. You can have this wonderful knowledge. Paul had it. He said "We," that is, I, "have the mind of Christ." God is no respecter of persons. He is as willing to reveal His mind to you, so far as you need it, as He was to reveal it to Paul.

4. But to possess this knowledge you must be holy. Sin darkens the understanding, and hinders the perception of truth. A grain of sand in the eye will prevent you seeing the most beautiful landscape in the universe, or the dearest friends you have. It is with the heart that men see divine things, and an atom of sin will darken the brightest vision that can come before you. With a pure heart you can not only see God's truth, but God Himself. Oh, God wants to reveal Himself to you. Will you let Him? But if He is to do so, you must have a clean heart.

VI. It is God's will that you should be holy, because He wants you to be men and women of courage. Courage is the most valuable quality in this War. There are few gifts of greater importance. Only think what it has enabled the Prophets, the Apostles, and the Salvation leaders of modern times to accomplish! How it covered Moses, and Joshua, and David, and Daniel, and Paul, and a crowd of others with glory, and enabled them to conquer men, and devils, and difficulties of all kinds. I shall have something more to say about this before I have done. Courage and Holiness are linked closely together. You cannot have one without the other. Sin is the very essence of weakness. A little selfishness, a little insincerity, a little of anything that is evil means condemnation, and loss of courage, which means cowardice and failure.

1. "The wicked flee when no man pursueth." Double- minded people are uncertain, fickle, unreliable in all their ways.

2. "The righteous are bold as a lion." Remember Shadrach, Meshach, Abednego.

VII. God wants you to be holy, in order that He may do mighty works through your instrumentality. I verily believe that His arm is held back from working wonders through the agency of many Officers, because He sees that such success would be their ruin. The spirit of Nebuchadnezzar is in them. He cannot build Babylon, or London, or New York, or anything else by their instrumentality, because He sees it would create the spirit of vainglory and boasting, or of ambition; make them dissatisfied with their position; or otherwise curse them and those about them. Look at Saul. What a lesson his history has in it for us all. "When thou wast little in thine own sight wast thou not made the head of the Tribes of Israel? and the Lord anointed thee king over Israel."

Section VII.

Now, I may be asked whether some Officers do not fail to reach the higher ranges of the experience I have here described, and the reasons for this. To this question I reply that I am afraid that it is only too true that some Officers are to be found who are willing to dwell in the land of uncertainty and feebleness. They are the slaves of habits they condemn in others. Their example is marred, their powers are weakened for their work, and, instead of going onward and upward to the victory they believe so gloriously possible, they are a disappointment to themselves, to God, and to their leaders. If I am asked to name the reasons for their neglect of this glorious privilege, I would say:

I. They have doubts about the possibility of living this life of Holiness. They think there is some fatal necessity laid upon them to sin — at least a little, or just now and then. They think that God cannot, or that He will not, or that He has not arranged to save them altogether from their inward evils. They know that the Bible says, over and over again, in a thousand different ways, that the Blood of Jesus Christ cleanses from all sin; and they read God's promise again and again, that He will pour out His Spirit upon them, to save them from all their idols and filthiness; but they doubt whether it is strictly true, or anyway, whether it applies to them. And so, tossed to and fro by doubts about this holy experience, no wonder that they do not seek to realise it in their own hearts.

II. Other Officers are kept back from climbing this mountain by the idea that the experience is not possible to them. They say, "Oh, yes, it is good, it is beautiful, I wish I lived up there. How delightful it must be to have your peace like a river, and your righteousness abound as the waves of the sea, and to be filled with the Spirit! But such a life is not for me." They admit the possibility of Holiness in those about them, and occasionally they push it on their acceptance, but they fancy that there is something about their own case that makes it impossible, or, at least, overwhelmingly difficult, for them to attain it.

1. They imagine that there is something in their nature that makes it peculiarly difficult for them to be holy. (a) Some peculiar twist in their minds. Some disagreeable disposition. (b) Some bad, awkward temper. (c) Some unbelieving tendency.

2. Or, they are hindered by something that they suppose to be specially unfavourable in their circumstances- their family.

3. Or, there is something in their history that they think is opposed to their living pure lives—they have failed in their past efforts, etc. Anyway, there is, they imagine, some insurmountable obstacle to their walking with Christ in white, and, instead of striking out for the summit of the Holy Mountain in desperate and determined search, relying on God's word that all things are possible to him that believeth, they give up, and settle down to the notion that Holiness of heart and life is not for them.

III. Then, other Officers do not reach this experience because they do not seek it; that is, they do not seek it with all their hearts.

1. They do not climb. They know that their Bible most emphatically asserts that those who seek heavenly blessings shall find them. No passage is more familiar to their minds or much more frequently on their lips, than the one spoken by Jesus Christ: "Seek, and ye shall find." And they condemn the poor sinner who lies rotting in the sins which will carry him to Hell, because he won't put forth a little effort to find deliverance. And yet, do not some Officers act very much after the same fashion with respect to this blessing? In their efforts they are truly sincere, but they are not much more forward for them. They say "It is not for me," and settle down as they were. The reason for this is not that the promise is not to them. But it is, (a) Because they have not been thorough in their surrender; or, (b) Because they have been wanting in their belief; or, (c) Because they do not

persevere; or (d) Because they have been mistaken in some past experiences.

2. Another reason why Officers do not find the blessing is the simple fact that they will not pay the price. There is something they will not do; or there is something they will do; or there is something they will not part with; there is some doubtful thing that they will not give up. The sacrifice is too great. They think they would not be happy, or someone else would not be happy, or something would not be satisfactory; and so they look and look at the Mountain, and long and long, but that is all. They would like to be there, but the price is too great.

3. Another reason why Officers fail is neither more nor less than their want of faith. This, with sincere souls, is by far the most common hindrance. I have something to say about faith further on.

IV. And, doubtless, the reason that some Officers fail to reach the upper levels of Mount Purity arises out of their mistaken views as to the nature of this experience. You have so often heard me dwell on this view of the subject that I despair of saying anything fresh that will help you. But, knowing that I am on ground where truly sincere souls are often hindered, I will make one or two remarks:

1. I have no doubt that many fail here by confounding temptation with sin. They pray, they consecrate, they believe that they receive, and they rejoice. But by-and-by, when bad thoughts are suggested to their minds, they say to themselves, "Oh, I can't be saved from sin, or I would not have all those wicked thoughts and suggestions streaming through my soul." They confound temptation with sin. Whatever they may say about it, they do not see the difference existing between temptation and sin.

2. Some Officers are hindered in the fight for Holiness by supposing that purity will deliver them from serious depression, low spirits, and the like. With many sincere souls I have no doubt that one of the most serious hindrances in this strife is the confounding of Holiness with happiness, and thinking that if they are holy they will be happy all the time; whereas the Master Himself was a Man of Sorrows, and lived, more or less, a life of grief.

V. Then there comes the last reason I shall notice, and that is the want of perseverance. There are some Officers who have been up the Mountain—part of the way, at any rate, if not to the top. But through disobedience, or want of faith, they have no longer the experience they once enjoyed.

VI. The condition. You say to sinners that they are never to give up. I do, at least. So with those who are seeking Holiness. They must persevere or they will never find it.

Chapter 4: The Spirit Of Devotion.

We now come to the message of the third Spirit. What was his message? What did he say? Listen: "*O Officers, Officers, you must be supremely given up to the saving of men.*" That is the great end for which The Salvation Army exists. On this message I remark:

I. That every man has some ruling, controlling object in life. That is, there is something which forms the chief attraction of his existence, and influences him most in all he feels, and says, and does in his everyday life. Perhaps he does not realise the presence or power of this force, or the influence it exerts over him, but it is there all the same.

II. That object constitutes his ideal. All the great things done by men are, in the first instance, simply ideals; that is, pictures in the mind, of what they would like to accomplish. And the realisation of these things by them usually comes about in something like the following fashion:

1. They see the thing in imagination.
2. They see that it ought to be done.
3. They see how it might be done.
4. They yearn after its being done.
5. They give themselves up to the doing of it. They say, "It shall be done, and I will do it, if it be possible." To illustrate what I mean take one or two of the achievements of human genius: the Suez Canal, the Alpine Tunnels. (a) In the first place, the idea was conceived. (b) The ways in which the idea might be accomplished were formulated. (c) The undertaking was resolved upon. (d) The work was embarked upon. (e) The task had to be persevered in. (f) Finally — but not until each of the other stages had been reached-the thing was triumphantly completed.

III. Now the real object for which The Salvation Army exists is known to us all. It is to save men. Not merely to civilise them. That will follow. Salvation is the shortest and surest cut to civilisation. Not to educate them. That will follow also; and if it does not, men and women had better live good lives, and get into Heaven at last, than, with heads full of learning, whether secular or religious, finish up in Hell. Not merely to feed them; that is good, very good, so far as it goes. It is true that in our Social work we feed the starving and house the homeless, but it is only a step towards the purpose we wish to accomplish. The object is to save men from sin and Hell. To bring them to God. To bring God to them. To build up the Kingdom of Heaven upon the earth. The end of The Salvation Army Officer is to convert men, to change their hearts and lives, and make them good Saints and Soldiers of Jesus Christ.

IV. And the Spirit of Devotion, with the crimson Cross inscribed upon his shoulders, who comes to us from the Throne of God, asks for our full consecration to the attainment of this object. Not merely that we should admire it, but really and truly choose it as the great end of our lives, and choose it afresh today. For this consecration certain things are necessary:

1. The knowledge of its nature. Many of you, I have no doubt, offered yourselves for a soul—saving life years ago. You knelt down, as I did, on the day you were converted—perhaps in the very act of being converted, and said, "Lord, help me to live for the salvation of those around me." But you have had much experience since then. You see what it means in the way of tears, of toils, of disappointments, of conflicts, to really follow the Lamb that was slain. What is asked from you by the Spirit from the Throne, is that with this increased knowledge and actual experience you should give yourself up to it again.

2. This consecration also implies a definite, intelligent offer of yourself to this object without reservation. This must be done in the face of all the possibilities before you, with all you really have and are, for better or for worse, and that for all your days. This consecration involves,

(a) The giving up of the pleasures and satisfactions that come from the world around you. For instance, (i.) The love of money. (ii.) The love of pleasure. (iii.) The love of admiration. The spirit, rather than the possession, of these things is the snare of the Officer.

(b) This consecration involves also a life of self-denial and toil. There is no other way. I say so.

3. Now, for the offering of ourselves to live and suffer for the salvation of the world after this fashion, we have the consecration of

Jesus Christ as an example. Look for a moment at what was involved in the offering He made for us. He foresaw all the humiliation, sorrow, suffering and mockeries that would have to be undergone, and the cruel death that crowned it all. And yet He voluntarily, and deliberately, and gladly gave Himself to the task. (a) It was voluntary. (b) It was made without regard to success or failure. (c) It was actuated by a motive which made it acceptable to God.

4. I doubt not that many Officers here have followed in His footsteps.

5. I hope it has been so with myself. I can remember making the offering for the first time sixty years ago. And I have told you before, how that, with the increased knowledge that came with years of suffering and toil, I made the offering in a fuller and more direct manner than at the onset.

6. Shall we go down before God, and ask ourselves whether after this fashion we are on the Altar this morning? And, if we are not, let us gladly place ourselves there.

Chapter 5: The Spirit Of Holy Warfare.

Section I.

The fourth Spirit who passed before us, is distinguished from the rest as the Fighting Spirit-the Spirit of Holy War. In his hand is a flaming sword, and the burden of his message, you will remember, was: *"O Officers, Officers, you must fight devils, lies, fleshly indulgences, hardships, disappointments, and everything that sets itself up against God, or that is opposed to the living of a holy life, or which threatens the damnation of man. O Officers, at all risks and consequences, you must fight for God and the salvation of souls."*

Let us look at this stirring and deeply interesting message.

I. And, first of all, what are we to understand by an Officer fighting? What does it mean? It means contending with oppositions-difficulties on every hand — doing, or struggling to do, what is hard to be done. When men get what they want without resistance, or loss, or suffering, they do not consider that to be fighting at all. In such circumstances they say, "There was no fight; it was a walk over." But when they have to struggle, when they have to meet opposing forces, when the conflict is desperate, and calls up all their powers, then they say it was a glorious victory when they win; and even when they lose, they reckon the loss is less to be mourned over if there was a real, a brave, a determined fight.

II. Now fighting is the common experience of men in this life. I do not know whether it will be so in the next. The general idea is that we shall have everything our own way there. The stream, they think, will run in harmony with our aims and wishes in the Celestial Land. I don't know whether it will be so. It will suit me if it does. Anyway, fighting is the order of the day in the present world. Whichever way you look, you will find that nothing is obtained without strife of one kind or another. The plants have to fight to bring their buds into flowers. The trees have to fight to bring their blossoms into fruit. The animals and birds have to fight, not only to avoid being devoured, but for almost every meal they eat. They would starve if they did not fight.

III. The whole life of man is little but a conflict.

1. There is the fight to get into the world.

2. There is the fight to keep living when you are in it. Look at it; at least one hundred millions of people have to fight to obtain food barely sufficient to keep body and soul together. Even then there are millions- forty millions in India alone —who are seldom free from the sensation of hunger. What a fight is theirs!

3. Look at the fight of still millions more with the diseases that wait to slay them at every turn. To them —indeed, in one sense, to us all— life is one long struggle with death.

4. Look at the fight men make for money. How they resist the claims of health and home, and fight against their own flesh and blood for gold!

5. Look at the fight men make for fame. See how they will sacrifice time, health, friends, nay, life itself, to get what they call a name. How they will glory in dying, as they term it, in the arms of victory.

6. Look at the fight men make for the governments they prefer.

IV. When you come to religion you will find this principle of conflict still more manifest. Here man will get nothing without a fight.

1. There are any number who will get nothing evil without fighting for it. For instance, a man cannot commit sin, mock God, trample on the Blood, resist the Holy Ghost, put out the eyes of his conscience, and die in despair, without fighting and a good deal of hard fighting too.

2. And if this applies to evil things, how much more to good things? Think of the struggle necessary to the attainment of any true spiritual advantage. For example:

(a) The moment a man starts to save his soul, difficulties of all kinds spring up before him. The past—how it holds on to him! The present—what a tearing away, and humbling, and confessing, he must go through! The future—how black and empty it often looks!

(b) He will have to fight to keep himself saved. Enemies will strive to destroy his new-born hope, and they will follow him to the very gates of Heaven to drag him down.

(c) He will have to fight if he is to save anyone else. Men cannot be turned from Satan to God by gentle phrases and lavender water. To save men is a desperate, agonising, wounding business.

(d) Think of the difficulties that have to be surmounted before a man can have ground for expecting the "Well done" at the judgment Throne, or a victorious crown in Heaven. "Be thou faithful unto death!" Do you ever consider what that faithfulness unto death meant to those to whom the words were first spoken? The visions of the torture chamber, the wild beasts in the arena, the Crucifixion, which it called up in their minds?

V. This fighting has always been a necessity when anything out of the common course in the way of the salvation of men has been sought after.

1. Read history. It would do some of you much more good than the halfpenny papers. Go to the prophets! What a fight Moses had! — Jeremiah—Jesus Christ—the Apostles—the Martyrs— the Reformers. My heart has ached many a time beyond description when I have read the biographies of the beautiful spirits who have wept, and fought, and laid themselves down to die without seeing the things accomplished for which they have suffered.

2. Fighting has ever been my own experience. From the beginning I have had to contend with earth or Hell, and sometimes with both, for every success God has been pleased to give me.

3. Fighting has been your experience. The day may come when the Salvation ship will glide along the stream of time, laden with souls bound for the Gloryland, without any pulling of the oars, or firing up of the furnaces, without any anxious lookout for stormy breakers ahead. But that time is not yet. Stop rowing, and you will see. Stop feeding the furnace. Stop fighting. You know what the result will be. If you are saviours of men you must fight. Make up your minds that it is so, and that nothing on earth or in Heaven, human or divine, can change it. The Devil has got possession of the world; anyway, of the people that dwell in it, and if you want them for Christ and holiness and Heaven, you will have to take your stand, and hold your post, and close with your enemy, and fight for their rescue; and you may be sure he won't loosen his grip without

inflicting all the damage he can upon you who dare to attack him and his prey. This law is not of my making. I am not responsible for it. I found it in my Bible when I first started to save myself and those around me, and it has been my experience ever since. It is God's plan and God's plan for us. Have you accepted it? I have. To do so is to go a long way to being happy in it—nay, to do so is to go a long way to being victorious.

Section II.

Salvation fighting, like all other warfare, seems capable of division into two parts. These two parts are so closely allied that it is difficult to treat them separately, and yet I must try to do so.

I. To begin with, there is the work that is necessary to keep the actual fighting going. This is, in reality, as much a part of the warfare as the actual attack on the enemy. Still, it often lacks the dash and change and excitement of the latter, and consists mainly of hard, monotonous out-of- sight toil. Such labour as this, however, is common to all warfare.

1. Not a hundredth part of the time of the military soldier, whether officer or private, is occupied with the excitement of battle, even in war time. All his other time and energies are taken up with doing uninteresting, monotonous, out-of-sight work. There is the drill. What an uninteresting set of repetitions that usually is! The guard—the watch, by day and by night. The long, weary marching, or the endless journeys by rail or ship; the carrying to and fro of ammunition; the preparation of the food: rough and ready as it often is, both officer and soldier are frequently glad if they can get any to prepare; the clothes to be kept whole; the cleaning of the weapons; the reporting of every movement of the enemy and of his own force; the doing of all these things must be very uninteresting, but none of them can be dispensed with.

2. Take commercial warfare, where you have much the same thing in both principle and practice. Think of the unceasing night and day work necessary to keep a railway running. Think of the monotonous work necessary to keep the doors of a big bank open, to construct a railway, make a tunnel, or a dock, or to conduct any similar operation. Work, work, work, is the order, the necessity of these and all similar transactions. They cannot be carried on without work.

3. This has applied to my own warfare. It is very easy to make a mistake here. You see me on the platform, you hear me talking to the thousands, etc. You say, "Ah, The General has a rare old time of it. He is sustained by a whirl of holy excitement. Bless him! Let us give him another volley! How different is his lot from mine!" But behind the scenes, out of sight, my body, and heart, and brain have to grind on night and day, and that with as little cessation as is the lot of any Officer in this Hall. I have not had a furlough for fifteen years. I have just decided to take a month on a motor car, but I am going to hold three meetings a day! But even if you still think my lot is more favourable, Lieutenant, than yours, in this respect, you must wait till you have ground on for fifty or sixty years as I have been enabled to do. Every man who wants to really lead must be willing to grind. It cannot be done without. It never has been. It never will be.

4. This rule applies to you, my comrades, if you are to be of any use to the world. You cannot be useful and successful without doing this uninteresting, out-of-sight work, and plenty of it.

5. You cannot have a battle without it. Think of the work some battles have involved. The monstrous toil of thousands of men for months, nay, years, in preparing for it. It is said that the Japanese had been preparing for the struggle with Russia for ten years. Some of you look upon this Congress-the public part of it-as a battle; and so it truly is, but think of the out-of-sight work that has been done to get ready for it; that had to be done if the battle had to be fought. Without the work you could not have had this glorious fight.

II. The Officer must do this kind of work, in order to prepare his Soldiers to fight. That is, he must deal with them as Soldiers. He must train them. One great difference between an Officer and a Soldier is the amount of Training that has been received. Not merely as bearers, supporters, contributors, collectors, admirers, but as Soldiers. How often have I told you this? I will tell you once more.

III. Every Officer ought to be encouraged by the consideration of the wonderful things that this monotonous kind of work has already accomplished. It is true that the public aggressive warfare has been largely instrumental in securing the remarkable success with which we have been favoured, but the steady out-of-sight labour has greatly assisted, not only in making that public fighting effective, but in conserving and consolidating the results. Take, as a definite illustration of my meaning, the work that has been involved in one branch of Army effort-the creation of our eighteen thousand Bandsmen. An immense amount of toil has been entailed in:

1. Getting them saved.
2. Watching over them.
3. Selecting them.
4. Teaching them.
5. Keeping them faithful.

Then look at the work they have had to do themselves in learning:

1. How to make the sounds.
2. How to read the notes.
3. How to keep the time.
4. The Italian and French words.

I heard of a drummer who used to take the drum to bed with him, and practise in the small hours of the morning.

Section III.

Now let me take the aggressive side of a Salvation Army Officer's life and warfare; and by that I mean the unflinching and fearless attack upon wrong-doing and wrong-doers. He must fight evil wherever and whenever he finds it. He must not let it alone. Tempted, though he will be, to say, "Let us have peace in our time, O Lord," he must unsparingly attack it. He must bring to that attack a determined mind, and a bold and loving heart. There will be two directions in which Officers will generally be required to meet and grapple with evil, and its consequences.

I. The first of these will be in the hearts and lives of the people entrusted to their care. There is a needs be that offences come. Jesus Christ said so. They cannot be prevented. They will be found, more or less, in every Command. Constituted as human nature is, even saved human nature, there will always be some trouble or evil to be faced by every real Commanding Officer and lover of souls.

1. The Officer must help his people in their fight with their own personal trials, temptations, and sins. He should make them feel that he is a real stand-by in their difficulties. Many of them are sorely tried.

2. Look at their depressions! How many of them go down into low spirits and despondency, and feel like giving up the struggle as hopeless. The Officer must fight that depression; He must encourage them, show them the bright side of the cloud, have patience with them. The balance of many a battle has been turned by one kind word, and thousands have been strengthened in the conflict with this kind of trial by the feeling that their leaders would cheer them up.

3. Look at the afflictions of the people! How few homes there are without sickness, and how few hearts without sorrow. Disappointment and loss and separation seem to be the common rule of the great mass. Look at the trials of parents in their children, and the trials of children in their parents. Remember the loneliness and separation of some wives and some husbands. And how many of our people all over the world are set alone in families and households far from their own loved ones. Now an Officer's duty is to help them in these trials. He is to get to know them, and give such advice as is helpful to them; stand firm as a rock by the side of those who are suffering, so that they may lean on him. In short, he must help them to fight their trials.

4. Look at the temptations of our people! Who can tell how many thousands of them have to struggle with the remnants of old habits, and the fiery temptations which come by old companionships, calling them back to evil? Look how many there are whose sorest temptations come to them through their families — young people especially, living in families all opposed to goodness. The constant butt of sarcasm and ridicule, and often tried beyond endurance. Consider how many of our Soldiers work amidst conditions which are simply abominable. Surrounded by blasphemy and filthy talk, or by the steady repulsive indifference of pride and hate. It is the Officer's business to help them to fight these evils.

5. Look at the spiritual foes of our people.

(a) Their weak natures. Do they not require help? It is no use blaming them. There they are, poor, wobbling, feeble creatures, many of them so by birth.

(b) Look at their wicked natures. It is no use disguising the fact. Many hearts seem unfavourable to the work of God's grace — stony, selfish natures. Twisted, awkward creatures, who go all through life taking everything and everybody awry. What a foe to a man's soul such a nature must be!

(c) Devils. Do we sufficiently realise that the devils are told off to destroy, and trip up, and overthrow? Every Officer here has some people under his care who are, this very day, being dogged, and pestered, and watched, and followed, with sleuth-like tenacity, by the fiends of Hell who are seeking to get hold of them. Now I say you are to fight these difficulties. You have not been saved and washed, and sanctified and called, and set apart and promoted, merely to record them, or to moan over them. All this has been done for you, that you may fight them with your own hands, and with your own hearts, and with your own strength of mind and soul. You must grapple with these evils. How can you better do this than you have done it in the past? That is the question. How can you more really conform to the command of the spirit of war than hitherto? Well, I can only give you one or two simple counsels, which I have found very useful in my own efforts to help the people around me. (i) Make them believe that victory is possible. And to do this, the most important of all is, that you should believe it yourself. Never let go your faith in the possibility of God's final triumphing in any soul you have to deal with. Say to yourself in the face of every weakness and disappointment, and say to them: "God can; God is able." Keep a smiling face. Many a battle has been won by the confident look of the general's countenance. Many a poor soul has been plucked from despair and damnation by the smiling face of his Captain in the hour of difficulty.
(ii) Do not let temporary defeats discourage them, or prevent them trying again. Forget the things which are behind. Show them how to do it. Never mind the disappointment you feel yourself. Do not show the white feather.

(iii) As far as possible deal with individuals. Give them personal advice which can only come by individual contact. Give all the instruction you can from your own experience. Stand up to families and employers who persecute your people. Visit them. Let them see your hearty interest in those for whom you plead. Sometimes you might take a deputation with you. Pray with them.

II. The second way in which Officers will be required to meet and grapple with evil and its consequences will be in fighting the

enemies of God and man who are raging and triumphing outside our camp. We all know the difference between the spirit of the Church and the spirit of The Army in this respect. The Church is ordinarily occupied with herself. As a rule, her clergymen, or pastors, or priests, do not feel any particular responsibility for the welfare of the people outside their own particular circle. It is true that by Missions—Home and Foreign—there is some attempt to reach the perishing multitudes, but these efforts soon crystallise into little churches themselves, becoming as formal and as separate from the perishing crowds as the mother who gives them birth. It is also true that, stimulated in a measure by the example of The Salvation Army, there has been, of late years, a great breaking out in Revival Efforts, Social Schemes, Forward Movements, and the like.

But, after all, the Church, as a whole, has little sympathy, and takes only a feeble part in these extraordinary efforts. And, if roused for the moment to consider the awful condition of the majority of mankind, she soon tires of toil and sacrifice on their account, and falls back upon her normal condition, which mainly consists in taking care of herself. She sustains her operations by her own gifts, and keeps up her membership by her own sons and daughters. But for the addition that comes to her from her own children and Sunday Schools, she would dwindle away and die. This method of sustentation is right, so far as it goes, and The Army will act on the same rule more than ever in the future.

SECTION IV.

I. You see the fiends of Hell, devouring the happiness and lives and souls of the people by thousands. I believe many of you do. I would to God you all did! You can see the Devil going about like a roaring lion. Are you willing to let those fiends feed on the bodies and souls of the people in peace? No! Then you must fight.

II. Again, you see around you the giant fiends of earth doing the same deadly work. Fouler fiends, I was going to say, are these fiends of earth than the fiends of Hell. There is pride; there is malice; there is worldliness in its unnumbered forms; selfishness; covetousness; drunkenness and the drunkard makers; harlotry and the harlot makers; infidelity and the infidel makers; hypocrisy and the hypocrite makers; war and the war makers. What will you do with them? What is the will of God that you should do with them? What does the message you have received from the Throne of God, this very Congress, say that you should do with them? You must fight them.

III. You must fight for the absolute rescue of these poor and deluded victims. Helping them is very good in many ways; but I am not quite sure of its advantages, if you leave them, still gripped fast in the clutches of the Devil. Anyway, you must not be content with: 1. Merely ameliorating their temporal miseries, or of delivering them from them. 2. Instructing them. 3. Changing their outward habits. 4. Attaching them to your Corps, or making them helpers in your work.

IV. You must not stop short of actually rescuing them from their sins, and changing their hearts, and making them into Soldiers of Jesus Christ. And how are you to do this?

1. You must do this by making the people know the truth. As regards God. Bring Him home to them. Make them realise that He is, and that His nature is Love, Justice, Purity. By making them realise the truth as regards sin. I have said something to you already about the search-light which He will give you. Now you must turn it on to people's consciences, and make them feel something of what He feels about their sinning against Him. By making them feel the truth as regards Judgment, Heaven, and Hell. All around you there is growing up a great peril of unbelief on these questions. You must fight it. You must make men feel and see that there is a Heaven, that there is a Hell, and that there will certainly be a great judgment Bar, before which they must stand. You must make them know the truth as regards the sacrifice of Jesus Christ and its sufficiency. Publish abroad the efficacy of the precious Blood, and all the blessings that flow from salvation.

2. You must do this by using all the means in your power to awaken men to their danger. Men sleep on the very verge of Hell. You must fight, to awaken them. They walk about in their sleep, and live as in a dream. Their business, their pleasure, their sorrows, their miseries, hold them fast in a slumber nearly as deep as death itself — nay, they are dead while they live.

You must awaken them, You know how you awaken people ordinarily who are asleep. You rush in upon them. You make them feel, hear, see something. You startle them, you change the current of their thoughts, you inflict a passing pain, or do something entirely unexpected. So here with these sleeping souls. You must do something. You must come in upon them in their business, and amidst their amusements. You must shake them in their sorrows, and in their bitter miseries. Startle them out of the fatal stupor in which they stand all unheeding on the brink of a burning Hell. Fight the sleeping sickness.

3. You must fight to make men repent. Not merely to listen to you and wish they were better, but to be sorry, angry with themselves, broken- hearted because they have been so wicked and so bad as to lift themselves up against God. He willeth not the death of a sinner, but that all men should repent. Your business is to fight for their repentance. You must do all this — amongst other means, by your own talking and appeals. Especially will this apply to your meetings. A satisfactory meeting, in my opinion, has always meant a real fight — a regular struggle to get something done at somebody for their good in time and in eternity. This applies no matter how large or how small the meeting may be. It should imply:

(a) A real effort to get the Devil out of some soul — young or old, rich or poor; to get God and goodness in; or to make somebody fight for Him who did not fight before. (b) This aim distinguishes me. (c) This aim distinguishes you. (d) This aim distinguishes The Army from the Churches around us. People they say fly from us. They won't come again. They are afraid of the attack. They don't like the plain dealing about their wrongdoing — the being brought face to face with their own conscience. This is true. No doubt they do. They fly from God. They fly from Jesus Christ. They quench the Spirit.

What then? We must fly after them. Anyway, we must go on with the work of rescue. The Dane who said, "My God! I never want to hear the Chief speak again." Shall the Chief hold back the truth, or soften his presentation of it because it cut into this man's guilty conscience. A thousand times, no! I say. What do you say? Does somebody here today ask me, "How shall I get the Spirit which produces this love and life of fighting?" Well, I would say, choose Him. Go down before Him here if you have never done it before and say, "O Blessed Spirit of the living God, Thou enemy of wrong, Thou who art the Eternal and unchanging foe of that great destroyer, Sin; Thou who hast drawn the sword, never to sheathe it again until Thine enemies become Thy footstool; I take my place beside Thee; I choose Thee as the captain of my soul; I give myself up to Thee, to drink in Thy Spirit, to conquer or to die."

Chapter 6: The Spirit Of Truth.

Section I.

We now come to the fifth Spirit—the shining Spirit of Truth. What was his message? Hear him again: "*O Officers, Officers, your work is to make men know the unchanging and the unchangeable truth about the love of God, the efficacy of the Blood of the Lamb, the accursedness of evil, the cruelty of the Devil, the terrors of the Great White Throne, the joys of Heaven, and the horrors of the damnation of Hell. To do this you must be filled with the Light yourselves.*"

I. You must know the things that are essential to a right and profitable discharge of the duties of your position.

II. Men perish in ignorance. You are sent to instruct them in the things that belong to their peace.

1. Men are blind. You must make them see. This is your duty. (a) You must make them see the evils of sin. (b) You must make them see the dangers of damnation. They go over the precipice because they don't see it. (c) They don't see the preciousness of the Divine favour. You must show it to them. (d) They don't see the beauty of believing. You must prove it to them.

2. Men are deaf. You must make them hear the voice of God calling them to His arms, imploring them to come and help.

3. Men are insensible to the charms of salvation. You must make them feel. This is your business.

III. To do this effectively you must be true yourselves.

1. You must yourselves know the meaning, and importance, and reason of the truths you proclaim to others. All the world over the cry is for more secular knowledge. Voices can be heard in all directions crying: "Give us more scientific knowledge, give us more technical knowledge, give us more knowledge about commerce and trade, give us more mechanical knowledge, give us more military knowledge." The cry is being attended to, and everywhere men and

women and children are hard at work with the prevalent answer to it. Men are learning how to construct machinery, explore the mazes of science, make fortunes, etc. There is no denying the fact that twenty years ago the Russians would have swept the Japanese off both sea and land in a very short time. What has made the difference? Knowledge. The Japanese now know as much, man for man, as the Russians, if not more. All that is necessary to be believed in order to your own salvation and the salvation of those about you with whom you have to deal, is already revealed. You do not require to study in order to discover the foundation principles that have to do with the salvation of the world. They are there, revealed and unalterable, for you to examine, receive, believe, and obey.

(a) For instance, we do not require any new revelation as to the Being of God, His nature and attributes, and the purpose He has in view in His dealings with men. Perhaps Enoch, and Moses, and John knew all that we know, and all that can be known down here.

(b) We do not require any new revelation respecting the person of Jesus Christ, His compassion, His miracles, His sacrifice, His resurrection and ascension, together with the virtue of His precious Blood.

(c) We do not require any new revelation respecting the Holy Ghost. His ability to purify and inspire the soul of man with the fire of burning love for a dying world is manifested.

(d) We do not require any new revelation about salvation itself, or the conditions on which it may be won, in order to share in the enjoyment of all its benefits.

(e) We do not require any new revelation about the consequences of the acceptance or rejection of God's mercy. We may have yet more light spread upon these joys and sorrows, but the great unalterable facts are there to accept or reject.

IV. But while we do not require any new revelation about Salvation, or its Author or character, there is room, nay, an absolute necessity, for definite improvement in the methods employed for its promulgation. The corn and oil carried from one part of the world to another are neither better nor worse than those precious commodities were in the Saviour's days. But there is a great improvement in the means of transit. I guess it would take Jacob's sons a longer period to traverse those couple of hundred miles between Canaan and the city of the Pharaohs than it now takes to bring corn to England from the western prairies of the United States or the north- western portions of Canada, a distance of five thousand miles or more. Suppose there had been anything like an equivalent advance in the method of spreading abroad the Bread of Life to that which has been made in the transmission of the natural staff of existence, the whole world would have been filled long ago with the song: "Glory to God in the highest." We must improve. It is true that great improvement has been made from time to time. For instance:

1. The Apostles were a great advance on the Prophets in the publication of Divine mercy.

2. The Salvation Army is undoubtedly a great improvement on the ordinary Christian organisations, both past and present, in the direction of conveying the saving knowledge of Divine grace to the sons of men. This is proved by her works, and admitted by the most thoughtful and experienced friends of God.

3. I trust that I am an improvement in the same direction upon many teachers and preachers who have preceded me. At least my people think so.

4. You are an improvement in the knowledge that makes men know and obey God, or you would not be here.

5. Greater improvement still must be possible. Surely, surely, we have not reached finality.

Section II.

Besides this improvement in the united operations of The Army, we want improvement in the individual Officer. With still further improvement in Officers we shall have improvement in every other direction. O Officers, Officers, you are my great concern. Were I dying before your eyes in this very Hall I should call on you, by all that was sacred on earth and in Heaven, to improve yourself. With many Officers there is unquestionably great advance. The Commissioners are improved, and so are the Staff generally. They are certainly dressed better, and from appearance I should judge they weigh much heavier. The Field Officers are improved, they do not appear to weigh any less. But there are other directions in which I think there is room for great improvement. On this subject there is room for a year's talking. But I will content myself with simply telling you something of what I would do for my own improvement, if I could go back to the days of my youth.

I. I would take more care of my health. Many of you have heard me speak about health, and tried earnestly and successfully to forget, at the earliest opportunity, the common-sense counsels I gave you on those occasions. Others, I have reason to know, profited by them; but alas! they are only the exceptions. I am able to speak to you experimentally. I have had difficulties on this matter all through my life. But until a serious attack of fever when I was sixteen, I scarcely knew what a day's sickness was. As far as my own feelings went I did not know that I had any digestive organs until then. I went on raging and tearing, outdoors and in, night after night, with long business hours, day after day, and long walks to preaching engagements on a Sunday. Then the breakdown came, and I have suffered in consequence ever since. Nevertheless, I am still in the same work. I am not going to say "Follow my example." I have no revelation, but my experience is an object-lesson which should, I think, be studied.

II. I would cultivate the habit of observation as a means of obtaining information. Not lazily allowing things to pass before my gaze without looking into them and asking myself, "How far can I profit by them?" But carefully studying men and women and children of all classes and conditions with a view of learning something from their badness and their goodness, their joys and their sorrows.

III. I would ask questions as I went along when I saw things that I did not understand. And not let everything pass as a matter of course unworthy of my thought and understanding.

IV. I would seek to strengthen my power of thought. Thinking is one great want of The Salvation Army at the present day. Officers do not sufficiently say to themselves, "Is there no way of doing this work more effectively? How can I improve on this plan? How can I better understand this truth?"

V. I would do everything that I reasonably could to improve my memory. Consider what some people have done with their memory. For instance, Spurgeon. Memory, like every other faculty, may be cultivated. You may readily, if you will inquire, get suggestions as to the cultivation of memories. But after all there is nothing like practice. One of the common snares is trying to do too much. I am not going to say that by any process you can improve your faculty to this extent. Still, a great deal can be done if you will make the effort, and you will find that the results will pay you well. Naturally, I don't think I excel with respect to this gift. Yet people often express their surprise at the extent to which I can call up things that I have heard and seen in the past.

VI. I would cultivate to its very utmost the habit of improving my time. One man says, "Time is dying, what can I do?" And there is an end of it, so far as he is concerned. Another lets the moments creep away without noticing any useful employment, without noticing their flight, or without feeling any regrets in consequence. This cultivation implies,

1. Some perception of the value of time.
2. The resolution to make the most of it.
3. What is most important of all, the habit of seizing the stray moments as they pass. This I have endeavoured to do until now. To be unemployed in some useful manner is absolute misery to me. But if I had my time to go over again I would go further still in this direction; in fact, I am doing so every day. I recommend the same to you.

Thomas Cromwell is said to have committed to memory the New Testament whilst travelling from London to Rome.

VII. I would seek that knowledge which before all others seemed most likely to be useful to me in my work of saving souls, and building up the Kingdom of Heaven. It cannot, in my opinion, be wise to spend time and energy in acquiring knowledge which has little or no bearing on the main object to which your lives have been specially consecrated, and for want of which souls are dying. Especially must this be the case with an Officer who is palpably ignorant on subjects of vital importance, intimately associated with successful labour, or who has capacities, which, if instructed, might do work of unutterable value.

The wandering mind. How few exercise control over their thoughts. I think I have to some extent been obedient to this law myself, but I would attend to it far more thoughtfully if I had my days to go over again.

VIII. I would read my Bible with greater regularity, and more carefully store my mind with its prominent histories, its most striking facts, and its most important teachings than I did in the days of my youth. That is a wonderful Book. The late Marquis of

Salisbury, for many years Prime Minister of this country, writing to a correspondent who had inquired his views of the New Testament, said:

"Everyone has their own point of view from which they look at things. To me the central point is the Resurrection of Christ, which I believe; first: because it is testified to by men who had every opportunity of seeing and knowing, and whose veracity was tested by the most tremendous trials, both of energy and endurance, during long lives; secondly, because of the marvellous effect it has had upon the world. To anyone who believes the Resurrection of Christ, the rest presents little difficulty. No one who has that belief will doubt that those who were commissioned by Him to speak— Paul, Peter (Mark), John—carried a Divine message. St. Matthew falls into the same category. St. Luke has the warrant of the generation of Christians who saw and heard the others. That is the barest and roughest form the line which the evidence of the inspiration of the New Testament has always taken in my mind. But intellectual arguments, as you well know, are not to be relied upon in such matters alone."

Another Prime Minister of England, the Right Honourable W. E. Gladstone, wrote a book upon the subject of the Inspiration of the Bible, to which he gave the title of "The Impregnable Rock of Holy Scripture."

IX. I would seek more industriously, as I had opportunity, to gather up in the storehouse of memory the leading occurrences in the world's history.

X. I would read with more care the biographies, and study the writings, of the men and women who have most closely walked with God, lived the holiest lives, been the most famous students of the science of soul-saving, and proved themselves to be the most successful heroes in that all-important warfare.

Section III.

Then I would more carefully cultivate the art, science, gift, or whatever you may call it, of speaking to men on the infinitely important subject of Salvation. Of the importance of this gift there is no need for me to speak to you. The Officer in The Salvation Army who does not see the grandeur of the opportunity he possesses of speaking to men about God and Eternity, and who does not earnestly desire to qualify himself for the effective discharge of the duty, must be altogether unworthy of his post. God has given me some ability as a public speaker. I have already referred to the tens of thousands I have been permitted to see kneeling broken-hearted at the mercy-seat. These thousands of souls all impressed, nay, deeply convicted and saved, bear witness to the power I possess as a salvation preacher. The Salvation Army itself is, to some extent, an evidence of my ability to talk to the hearts of men. Am I glorying in myself? God forbid. I say these things for your sake, to justify me in advising you in listening to my counsel. Now how did I acquire this ability to talk? Beyond question I possess some natural gifts — they came into the world with me. But for the encouragement of every young Officer here today, I want to say that the bulk of my little ability as a public speaker has come by the way of industrious, persistent, self-denying cultivation. My soul was drawn out in desire after the power to speak of the things of God to the hearts of men in the earliest hours of my first love. I yearned after it with an unutterable yearning, and that long before I had any reason to believe that this gift would ever be mine. I made up my mind to seek it before I had been saved twelve months, and at once set myself to the task. I have fought hard in this pursuit. Few Officers here have had more disappointments, and depressions, and temptations in their talking than I have myself. But I have persevered, and I am still following on as earnestly as ever in the pursuit. But I never expect to reach satisfaction with my attainment in this respect, and so shall still fight on to gain greater ability to persuade men to abandon the path of evil and seek God; to save souls, and help Jesus Christ to win the world, till I drop into the grave, and exchange earth for Heaven. Does anyone ask me how I have attained what ability as a talker I do possess? I answer that I am coming to the opinion that every man must learn for himself how to talk, if ever he learns at all. However, I will give you a few hints. And I will do so by describing the things which, taken together, are likely to make a successful Salvation Army talker.

I. He must be actuated by right, God-pleasing motive: Almost everything will depend on the character of the motives which carry him to the people.

1. His aim must be beyond all self-seeking — vain, man-pleasing feelings. If he is after the praises of men, or the rewards of this world, he cannot expect the Holy Ghost to second his efforts.

2. His motive must be above the mere desire to preach the truth or explain the Bible, or remind his hearers of what they already know. In these things there is no practical application of truth to the present need of those before him.

3. His aim must be to bless them by saving them in some form or other from sin, and leading them on to a more earnest, self-denying life for God and the salvation of others.

II. Having this aim, much will depend on preparation for the right discharge of the duty. There are different views on the subject of preparation for the platform. I will tell you mine. Some think that no preparation is needed; that it is wrong to pray and study as to the message you are to deliver. "Open your mouth wide," they say, "and God will fill it." That is not my view, and it has never been my practice. To those who entertain these notions I would say: If you are on such good terms with the Blessed Spirit that He will fill your pitcher with the living water without any trouble to yourself, very good. I have always had to draw mine out of the well, and very deep I have often found that well to be; and very hard pumping it has usually been to get out what I have wanted. It is true that many of my most impressive, most convincing, and most effective thoughts, illustrations, and appeals have come to me on the platform at the moment they were needed. But, as a rule, I have had to work my brain, search my Bible, look over my experience, call up to memory the incidents of the past, and then, with infinite pains, cast these thoughts, etc., into shape, and fix them into such order as has seemed most likely to produce the effect I have desired on the hearts of my hearers. It is true that in nature every now and then you will have a good crop in your garden for which little or no preparation has been made; but is that any rule why you should give up cultivating altogether? Just so with talking. Do you ask me how I would advise an Officer to go about preparing an address? As I have said, I have tried before, and with little success, and now I have little time. Here, however, is an outline:

1. Choose your subject. Your subject should in some way be-

> (a) Applicable to the present need of the people who will hear you. Very much alike.
> (b) Practical—something that can be turned to present account.
> (c) Interesting, if possible. Something that will catch the ear, and move the curiosity at once.

111

(d) Within your ability to handle.

(e) One on which you can ask God's endorsement and blessing.

2. Having chosen your subject, consider the form in which you can best present it.

3. Explain the truth you present in the simplest language you can find. Avoid the common error of talking over people's heads. Use your own language, such words, that is, as you are accustomed to employ when expressing yourself in the affairs of your everyday life.

4. Make certain that you are understood by the most ignorant of your hearers; illustrate freely. The simpler your illustrations are the better. Illustrations that need explanation are next door to useless.

5. Support what you have to say, so far as you can, by facts. Nevertheless, don't drag yourself in more than advisable.

6. Apply the truth preached as you go along.

7. Appeal for action corresponding to what you have been urging on your hearers there and then. "Now is the accepted time."

Section IV.

And now that you have got your topic, and prepared yourself for it, what about the manner of its delivery? Well, I have been describing it as I have gone along. Another word may be useful. I will tell you what I think you should aim at:

1. Aim at naturalness. Be yourself. Don't mimic anyone else. If you are yourself you will be sure to be interesting. This is difficult, strange to say, but you must struggle after it.

2. Aim at distinctness. As a rule, your bearers will not be at much trouble to listen to you, and therefore must know what you are saying, that is, what you mean, without having to attend very closely. That is, if they are to be any forwarder for your talk.

3. Aim at directness. Talk to the people. Beauty is said to be the eye of the beholder. I get my inspiration out of the eyes of those who listen to me.

4. Be in dead earnest. This is the crowning quality of all Salvation talking. You have all heard of the orator, who, when asked

what were the chief properties needed for effective public speaking, replied: "Action, action, action." I can hardly believe it, but if anyone proposed the question to me in its reference to a Salvation Army speaker, I should say: that, given something to say, the all-important thing needed is—earnestness, earnestness, earnestness. Now that is my counsel with respect to your improvement. Standing here, as I do, with nearly sixty years of experience and observation behind me; with my mind open before Heaven to receive further light direct from Him or through any medium; and desiring, with an unutterable desire, to rightly interpret the mind of God as it may affect the important questions we have been considering, I do not think that any more useful or practicable advice could very well be given you. May God help you to act upon it.

Spread the light. You have it. What is the use of a sun that does not shine?

Chapter 7: The Spirit Of Faith.

Section I.

And now we come to the sixth of these wonderful Spirits, the Spirit of Faith. Each Spirit that has passed before us from the Throne of God, in this Congress, has brought us a message of unutterable importance, but none has a closer bearing upon our holiness, usefulness, and joy than the one whose message we now come to consider, viz., the Spirit of Faith. It is important to us personally; to God's Kingdom; to the whole world; and to our work in the world. Let us hear that message again: "*O Officers, Officers, you cannot do without me. Listen to my words. If you treasure them in your hearts, and carry them out in your lives, you shall be conquerors. If you neglect them, you will be defeated, no matter how brave you are in other things. You must take the inscription on my banner as your life-long motto – You must believe. You must do it night and day, in sorrow and in joy, in defeat and in victory, living and dying. You must be men and women of faith.*"

Let us proceed to consider this counsel. And, first, I remark:

I. How desolate we should all be without faith, no matter what else we possessed, either of this world or any other.

1. It is only by means of faith that we can obtain any satisfactory assurance of the existence of God. To be without faith, then, is to be without God. That is, "without hope, and without God in the world." It is true that there are voices in nature and voices in Providence, and voices within us, and voices that come from the good and true around us that are ever saying, "There is a God;" but unless we believed their testimony all would be in vain. Anyway, they would do little more than land us in the desolate swamps of uncertainty on this all-important question.

2. But, while accepting the fact of the Being of God, it is only by faith that we know that He has spoken to man. Therefore, to be without faith would be equivalent to being without a Bible. What that loss would be it is difficult to conceive. Suppose we woke up tomorrow morning, and found that every Bible at present in

existence had been taken out of the world? Or suppose—which would amount to the same thing—that, all at once, we discovered that every page in our Bibles had become blank paper? What a mourning and lamentation there would be, and justly so. People who had never thought it worth the trouble to read their Bibles would wail. People who had read, and disbelieved would mourn. Even people who had read and disobeyed would feel they had lost what could never be replaced. And yet, to have the Bible without a living faith in its revelations, and a positive obedience to its precepts, is really worse than having none at all. For he that reads his Maker's will, and believes it not, is not likely to obey; and to know and not do is to be visited with the greater condemnation.

3. It is only by faith that we can obtain any assurance of an existence beyond the grave. To be without faith is, therefore, equal to being without immortality. Men may make guesses, and indulge in aspirations in favour of a future life, but without faith there is no assurance on the subject. They are left to imagination. It is only by faith that we know that we are of any greater value than the beasts of the field—anyway, so far as existence after death is concerned.

4. It is only by means of faith that we can obtain any satisfying assurance of the favour of God.

5. Without faith there can be no real peace amidst the trials, conflicts, and agonies of life. All the attempts of philosophy to manufacture consolation in such circumstances have proved a dead failure. They have been tried. They are a mockery, a delusion, and a snare.

6. To be without faith is to be without any true ground of hope for the future. It is only by faith that we have any reasonable ground for expecting any happier state of things in the new world than we have in the present.

7. To be without faith is to have no Calvary, no Saviour, no forgiveness. We only know that Jesus died for our sins, and lives again to save us from them, through believing in God. Indeed, without faith in Him life must be a dismal wilderness, and the future a dark, starless blank.

II. Not only is faith the only medium by which we can come to know and realise spiritual things, but the measure of our faith will generally be the measure of that realisation. In other words, the religious life of an Officer will be governed by his faith. Salvation is commenced by means of faith, maintained by faith, and brought to a triumphant issue by faith.

1. Your conversion was by faith.
2. Your assurance of it has been received by faith.
3. Your peace and gladness have been according to your faith.
4. Your usefulness in honouring God and saving men has been, and will be, according to your faith.
5. Your triumph on your dying bed will be according to your faith.
6. Your crown, happiness, honour, and reward in Heaven will depend upon the extent to which the Spirit of Faith has led you, and enabled you to do all the holy will of God. (a) If you have but a little faith, a half-starved, neither-hot- nor-cold affair, you will only have a little salvation. (b) If you have a bigger, bolder, stronger faith, you will have a bigger, grander, more glorious salvation. (c) If you have a full measure of faith, that is, if like Stephen and Barnabas of old, you are full of faith, and of the Holy Ghost, you will have a full measure of salvation. That is, you will have salvation up to the full limit of your capacity and need: "Good measure, pressed down, shaken together, and running over." All this is in harmony with the law laid down by Jesus Christ when He said, "According to your faith be it unto you."

Section II.

The doctrine specially insisted on by the Spirit of Faith must be of great interest to Officers of The Salvation Army, because it may be truly said to govern their success. Faith will have to do with the measure of your success; indeed, that success will be largely determined by the measure of your faith. Other qualities and gifts will certainly be required. For instance, an Officer's success will be assisted by natural gifts and conditions; such as,

1. Good health.
2. Pleasant appearance. Beauty, comeliness, etc., will attract and impress; but here we are all at an advantage.
3. An agreeable voice.
4. Fluency in talking.
5. Intelligence.
6. Special gifts. But all these put together will be of little service without faith. Indeed such gifts, without faith, are often a hindrance rather than a help. For, with a simple earnest faith, an

Officer may do a thousand times more for God and souls without these advantages than he will do with them all, if he has no faith.

For, consider,

I. An Officer's success will largely depend upon his faith in himself.

1. This will apply to his personal realisation of the experience he urges on others. If he is uncertain as to whether he himself possesses the Salvation he pushes on his bearers, his trumpet cannot be expected to do any other than give an uncertain sound. To be doubting and fearing about himself while he is talking will mean weakness and failure in all he says.

2. His success will also depend upon his faith in the consistency of his life with the standard he holds up before others.

II. The faith of an Officer in The Army will have much to do with his success. It is so with me. You all know how I feel about The Army. You all know that I believe in it, and that faith helps me to study, and write, and travel, and pray, and talk, and govern. I feel that it is worth all the effort I can make. That faith cheers me in success, and comforts me in disappointments and defeat. I say to myself of a particular effort or special meeting, "If this is not as effective as I desire, it cannot prevent the onward march." For instance: If you only know and believe in The Army's history, I am sure you will fight for it. Ditto, its principles. Ditto, its system and future. If an Officer finds himself in doubt about a Leader, or an appointment, what shall he do? Run away? No. Even if he had a General whom he did not trust, what then? Should he give up, and run away? No! Hold on, have faith in The Army.

III. The measure of an Officer's faith in the comrades around him will have much to do with his success. If you believe in them, that faith will strengthen and comfort your heart. The thought that brave, true hearts and hands are fighting with you for the same blessed truths will be an undying stimulus. To believe that they will carry forward the work you are struggling over, when you are battling elsewhere, or when you are gone to your Heavenly Home, will be a strength to your heart. Even if there are some bad—one in so many—they were once good. But even where you have faults believe in the good in them. This is the principle that makes the

Soldier's relations to his General so valuable. How many do your people count you for?

IV. The success of an Officer will be largely influenced by his faith in the high value of what he fights for. You cannot succeed without hard, self-denying, cross-bearing work. And whether you do that work heartily or not will largely depend on the estimate you set on the value of the men and women for whom you fight. If you think they are of little more value than the animals around you, you won't be very willing to suffer or sacrifice very much to save them. Who would die to save an ox or a sheep?

A recent number of "V.C." has the following:

"The Lass from The Army."

"She was a Salvation Army lass, and her lot was a hard one. Working from seven in the morning till six o'clock at night, weaving hair-cloth, she was dull and poorly-paid work, but in addition she had to bear the constant and thoughtless gibes of her fellow-workers. One autumn morning a spark from a bonfire on some adjoining allotment gardens entered an open window, alighted on a heap of loose hair, and the next minute the place was ablaze. A rush for safety of the work-girls followed. 'Is everybody down?' asked the foreman. His question was answered by one of the weavers, who, holding up a key, shrieked, 'My God! I locked Lizzie Summers in the piece shed for a joke not a minute ago! The piece shed was a room to be reached only through the burning building, through which it seemed impossible to make way. Girls and men were standing aghast and helpless, when two figures stumbled through the smoke which poured from the weaving-room. One was seen to be Lizzie Summers; the other was, for the time, unrecognisable. It was The Salvation Army lass. She had stayed behind, burnt, blistered, and half-suffocated, to batter down the door in order to liberate and save the life of her coarsest-tongued tormentor."

If you don't think that the people are of any great worth you won't be likely to face either fire or water to save them. But if you believe-

1. That they are immortal, that they will live for ever.
2. That their souls are of indescribable worth.
3. That God loves them, and wants to get them into Heaven.
4. That Christ thought them of sufficient value to lay down His life for them.

5. That they are every hour in peril of the wrath of God and the damnation of Hell. If you believe all this, or a reasonable part of it, you will work, and weep, and pray, and fight to save them. Believe! Believe! If you do not believe you will only go as far in the effort that brings success as you are forced, by custom, or orders, or salary, or the good opinion of the dying nobodies about you. If you believe a little, you will fight a little. If you believe much, you will fight much.

Richard Cecil, one of the great soul-winners of bygone days, in words which produced a great effect on my own heart, said: "Faith is the master spring of the minister. Hell is before me and thousands of souls shut up there in everlasting agonies; Jesus Christ stands forth to save men from rushing into this bottomless abyss; He sends me to proclaim His ability and love. I want no fourth idea! Every fourth idea is contemptible! Every fourth idea is a grand impertinence!"
Faith will determine what you are and what you do.

V. The success of an Officer will be largely influenced by his faith in the means he employs to secure that success. For example:

1. His faith in the doctrines he preaches will have to do with his success. If he does not really believe in them, they will have little effect on his own heart, and consequently little effect on the heart of anyone else. But if he has received them into his own soul, if they are realities to him, they will move him, and, moved by them, he will move the people he talks to. Especially if his own faith is "mixed with faith in them that hear" his message. For instance: if he sincerely believes -

(a) That there is a glorious Heaven.
(b) That there is an awful Hell.
(c) That there is going to be a Judgment Day.
(d) That Jesus Christ came down and died for men.
(e) That the miseries of the people before and around him can be cleared away by the power of God, his own soul will be so moved.

2. His faith that the truths he proclaims apply to the persons to whom he proclaims them. If he believes that the truth of the doctrines he preaches will take hold of the very people present at that particular time he will be likely to pour out the truth. If he is quite sure that what he has to say about conscience, and death, and

judgment, and Hell will shake the souls of the sinners who sit before him there and then, whether they be few or many, he will be likely to talk effectually, whatever the nature or size of the meeting may be. One great reason for the marvellous power my dear wife had over the audiences she addressed was her confidence in the truth she had to preach, and in her particular manner of presenting it. "Only get them to hear me," she would say. Right or wrong, that was her notion.

3. His faith in the methods he employs will also influence his success.

(a) To begin with his method of working the Open-air. The Officer who does not believe in the value of the Open-air will not be likely to get much out of it. If he only regards it as a call-bird for the indoor services he will probably be content with little more than a performance. Whereas the Officer who goes for converting the people on the spot, appealing to them as they stand there, and arousing and awakening their consciences, will be likely to make his Open-air a means of great blessing to Soldiers and sinners alike. I always believed in the Open-air — hence, perhaps, my success with it.

(b) The method of conducting his indoor meetings and of carrying on all the other departments of his work, whether his visitation, his singing, his talking, his fishing, his penitent-form, or anything else. Without faith they will all be heartless performances — a kind of play-acting. David believed in his sling and his stones, and Goliath was as good as dead before he got at him. No doubt David's method was good, and likely to succeed, but it would have been useless to David if he had not had faith in it.

VI. An Officers success will be largely influenced by his faith in the actual co-operation of God with him. For instance, consider the effect on all he is, and says, and does, if he earnestly believes among other things:

1. That there is a Holy Ghost. I think sometimes that the practical belief in the existence of the Holy Ghost distinguishes The Army Officer from other workers around him.

2. Again, consider the effect upon an Officer's feelings and work by a practical belief that the Spirit delights to help Officers who are striving to save and sanctify men. If a son was striving in a far

country to know and carry out the father's law, he could rely on the father's help.

3. Consider also that the Holy Spirit is with him while engaged in his efforts for God and souls whatever those efforts may be. We all know how strong and brave the company of those we love or reverence makes us in times of trial and conflict. With what courage must a firm belief in the presence and co-operation of God inspire an Officer in the fight.

VII. It may sound strange, but there can be no question I think, that a real faith in the actual presence and opposition of a personal Devil will help an Officer. It is a real opposition. To believe that the Devil is present and actually engaged in opposing you, will account for many things that frequently transpire in connection with an Officer's work. How you feel if the Split Band is after a Bandsman! If the next Corps Treasurer is after a shopkeeper in your High Street for Self-Denial, though he did not give to you last year. Well, here is a roaring lion — a fiery serpent.

For instance:

1. Take the silly trifling of hearers that you see sometimes. That can be put down to the Devil. Not always.
2. Take the unreasonable going out of hearers. You can put that down to the Devil. Not always.
3. Take the bad-tempered and unreasonable opposition that often has to be encountered. You can put that down to the Devil. Not always.

VIII. An Officers success will be very much influenced by the faith he has in results. It is a Spirit. They say that nothing succeeds like success. Anyway, it is difficult to secure success without faith.

1. To believe in defeat is to bespeak defeat.
2. To be afraid that nothing will happen is to make it very likely that nothing will happen.
3. To believe that you will win is to make it very likely that you will win, and that because it will ensure the doing of your very best to secure it.

Your faith or your unbelief will influence the faith or unbelief of those about you. How eagerly the officers and soldiers watch the face of the General when a battle is going on. If they think he is confident, then they will be confident too, and fight accordingly. So that with a strong faith in victory, the battle is half-won before a blow is struck.

Section III.

I. I want to close this address by the mention of one aspect of the work of the Spirit of faith which appears to me to be specially important to Salvation Army Officers. In point of order it ought to have been mentioned earlier on, but in view of its peculiar interest, I have reserved it to the close of my observations on the subject. The subject to which I refer is the influence that Faith is intended to exert on an Officer's peace of mind amidst the varied and frequent trials with which he usually has to contend.

II. I need not say that an Officer's peace of mind is intimately connected with his holiness and usefulness. That you all know full well, and on that ground you will know also how desirable it must be.

III. Officers have very many trials, some of which are at times very severe. We all have—I have trials myself—my life has been a continued series of trials. And so it is with many of my dear Officers.

1. There are personal trials.

(a) Those that relate to the body.
(b) Those that relate to the mind.
(c) Those that relate to the spirit.

2. There are family trials—husband, wife, children, two sets of relatives, two mothers-in-law. If you don't want trials don't marry.

3. There are trials arising out of appointments that do not appear to fit in with our notions, and which are often very perplexing. Corps, Comrades, success and failure, and many other things.

IV. No one can claim exemption from trials.

V. Counsels without number of different kinds have been Propounded for dealing with trials and sorrows.

1. The Stoical Spirit says Hide, endure.
2. The Spirit of the Coward says, When you can bear your sorrows no longer, run away, resign, despair, commit suicide.

3. The Rebellious Spirit says, Complain, murmur, turn infidel, kick against the pricks. This does not answer.

4. The Worldly Spirit says, Drown your sorrows, music, pleasure, intoxicants, opiates.

5. Then Reason says, (a) These things may be working out your own benefit. Educating you for a higher sphere of honour, etc., on earth or in Heaven. "For our light affliction, which is but for a moment, worketh for us a far more exceeding and eternal weight of glory." (b) Reason on the subject. Look around and you will always find someone worse off than yourself. (c) The good of others—extend salvation. (d) Faith says: Trust in God. These trials are all known to God; indeed they are all known to Him. By His direct appointment, or by His permission. Perhaps could not help Himself "It comes from above." My own experience is my late trials. "Peace, doubting heart."

Chapter 8: The Spirit Of Burning Love.

Section I.

I. And now we come to the consideration of the message of what is, beyond question, the most attractive of the seven beautiful Spirits who are before the Throne of God, and who have occupied our attention these few days; namely, the Spirit of Love. His form will long linger before your eyes, and His message will tremble on your ears, for many a day. What was the message that he brought? Let me repeat it: *"O Officers, Officers, commissioned by the Great 'I Am,' I come to tell you that in all you think, or speak, or do, Love must be the ruling passion of your lives."*

You must love each other. You must love your Soldiers. You must love poor sinners. You must love God. And that not after a tickle, cold, half-hearted fashion, but with a changeless, quenchless, Burning Love.

Now I want to remark on this message:

1. A widespread visitation of love is more needed by our poor undone world than all else beside. The vast majority of its inhabitants are hopelessly sinking down in slavery, debauchery, idolatry, and all manner of iniquities. These things lead to every kind of wretchedness in this life and in the life to come. Luxury, law, wealth, science, learning, and no end of other human contrivances have failed to remedy this state of affairs, and will fail. Love is the remedy. Here is the Divine panacea, this is the recipe for the millennium: love. Divine love. Oh, for a deluge of this blessed spirit!

2. My second remark is that a baptism of Divine Love is the great need of the Officers assembled at this Congress. I am sure that above, and beyond all else, my soul longs for a fresh and more powerful visitation of this blessed, fiery flame. In this desire I feel certain that the hunger of hundreds, nay, thousands of hearts here present, is in harmony with my own.

3. I want to speak to you, therefore, with all the plainness and affection of which I am capable on this subject. I am now rapidly nearing the end of my counsels to my Field Officers. Doubtless, you think the best wine ought to come last. I think so myself, and in this subject I feel that that requirement is fully met, and it has the advantage of being equally applicable to my comrades, both on the Staff and in the Field.

4. Divine Love is a charming theme, presenting an occasion for unending discussion, but my time will only allow me to give it a passing glance. For a few moments, therefore, I must ask your consideration of the effect that must inevitably follow in the heart and life of an Officer who is inspired with the all-absorbing passion of Burning Love.

II. I need not say that the Love of which I am going to speak is the pure, unselfish affection. I leave out of our inquiry the human sentiment often spoken of by the term love, and which has no moral character in it. That is a mere instinct at its best, differing little from that possessed by the animal creation around us, and cannot be said to have either praise or blame attached to it. The love which would make a bear fight to the death for her cubs is of the same level with that which would make a mother die for her children. I am simply going to deal with that Holy, Celestial Flame, which, emanating from the heart of God, unselfishly seeks the highest well—being of its object, both for this world and the next.

III. This love, like every other emotion of the human heart, can be experienced in varying degrees.

1. There is a love that is lukewarm. True love, beyond question, it often is, and unselfish too, but so feeble as to be scarcely worthy of the name.

2. There is a love that is fickle and spasmodic. Hot and ready to promise, to do, and to be, and suffer today, but cold, and powerless, and all but extinct tomorrow.

3. Then there is the steady, earnest, burning passion, which, whatever feelings may come or go; whatever advantages may promise, or whatever threatenings may frown, is ever the same overpowering principle in the soul. That is what I call "Burning Love," and that is for a few minutes my theme. On it I want to say something practical and useful. How can I do so? Oh, Thou Great God of Love, help me to speak of this, Thine adorable nature, so that

I may draw out the hearts of my comrades more than ever. To wonder and admire, and to seek to have their own souls filled, absorbed, and mastered, by the celestial passion that fills, absorbs, and masters Thine.

Section II.

Burning love in the heart, life and character of an Officer will compel him to feel, and do, and safer many things.

I. Among other things it will lead to the adoration and worship of God.

1. By worship I mean that admiration of, and thanksgiving to the Divine Being, which ought to be realised in the hearts, and manifested in the lives, of all His intelligent creatures.

2. God ought to be worshipped. He is so great, so powerful, so good and so loving, that every being, and everything that His hand has made, ought to bless and praise Him. The Bible abounds with exhortations to worship.

3. We expect to worship Him in Heaven. To bow before His Throne, to offer Him the overflowing thanksgiving of grateful hearts, to join in the blood-washed multitude, whom no man can number, in chanting His praise, will, taken together, constitute, we anticipate, a large portion of the rapture of that Holy Place.

4. We ought to worship Him on earth. I think sometimes that The Salvation Army comes short in the matter of worship. I do not think that there is amongst us so much praising God for the wonders He has wrought, so much blessing Him for His every kindness, or so much adoration of His wisdom, power, and love as there might, nay, as there ought to be. You will not find too much worship in our public meetings, in our more private gatherings, or in our secret heart experiences. We do not know too much of

> *"The sacred awe that dares not move,*
> *And all the inward Heaven of love."*

Many reasons might be assigned for this if there were time. To some extent its absence can be excused. Still, it is a cause for regret. Burning love will remedy the defect. To love more will be to worship more.

5. One condition of worship is acquaintance. You must know something of the good qualities of a being before you are likely to

admire and adore him. There must be a knowledge of God before the soul will prostrate itself in worship at His feet. The soul that loves God will seek His presence, delight in His communion, dwell on His perfections, and, filled with rapture by their contemplation, fall before Him and wonder and adore. Burning love will worship.

6. Gratitude is another quality essential to worship. "I thank Thee" is the first language love learns to lisp. The smallest favours bestowed by the object loved are not only noticed but magnified. Burning Love delights to bow before the Saviour and sing: "Oh, let me kiss Thy bleeding feet," etc.

7. Praise is another element of worship. The Psalmist says, "Whoso offers praise glorifies God." That is, makes Him more to be admired and famous in the eyes of angels and men.

Burning Love never tires of sounding forth the praises of the object loved.

(a) It praises Him, and His wonderful works, and all around.
(b) It lies before Him, and speaks them in His own listening ear. The language of Burning Love is: "I'll praise my Maker while I've breath, And when my voice is lost in death Praise shall employ my nobler powers. My days of praise shall ne'er be past, While life, and thought, and being last, Or immortality endures." But worship means more than either realisation, appreciation, gratitude or praise; it means adoration. The highest, noblest emotion of which the soul is capable. Love worships.

II. Burning Love will promote your resemblance to God. As I have said, love is largely made up of admiration. What the soul admires it imitates, whether intending to do so or not.

1. This is said to be the case physically. I have heard it said that the love existing between husbands and wives leads to their resemblance of each other in bodily appearance.

2. We see it mentally every day.

3. We know it so morally. The company and example of good men make good men, or ought to do. So, if you love God with this burning passion, you will, you must grow like unto Him.

III. Burning Love promotes obedience. We have all heard it said that love is a slave, which means that the lover delights to do the will of the beloved. It does not have to punish itself; nor to be punished, to make it carry out the wishes of the object loved, so far as it has the ability. So, when the soul loves God, "I delight to do Thy will."

IV. Burning Love opens to the soul new and overflowing sources of unspeakable joy.

1. To begin with there is the joy of loving. The chief satisfaction arising from love is found not in being loved, but in loving.

2. In order to realise the true satisfaction of love, there must be love in return. A man finds no satisfaction in the love of his wife when he has ceased to love her in return, and given his affections to another woman; in fact, then he would rather she did not love him. Her love is a torment to him, because he has ceased to love her. Just so with the love of God for us. If we do not love Him back again, we have no pleasure; but if we give Him our hearts, we find unutterable pleasure in the love He bore to us.

3. The measure of the joy imparted by loving is proportionately increased by the greatness, and goodness, and beautifulness of the object loved. Think of loving God! "The bliss of those who fully dwell."

V. Burning Love will make the Officer the true friend of mankind. He will love men and the things of men. That is, he will unselfishly care for their well-being for their own sakes. There is lawful and unlawful love as regards the things of this life:

1. The love of wrong things.
2. The wrong love of right things. The love of God and the things of God need not lessen an Officer's lawful love for the lawful things of earth. It will purify and often strengthen that love, and make it a happier love than it was before. For, with this purified affection,

(a) He will love the things of nature. Rivers and hills and trees and seas will now be marks of his Father's wisdom. He will love the lovable; it will be his nature to do so. His God took pleasure in creating them. He takes pleasure in them today. It is lawful for His children to take pleasure in them also.

(b) With this love he will love the people about him. His family, husband, wife, lover, friend.

(c) With this love he will love the poor, the suffering, the weak, the hungry, the sick. He will compassionate them. He will go after them, and touch them, and take them by the hand, etc. He will follow Jesus Christ's example, as described in the New Testament. Take out from it the Hospital, the Shelter, the Food Depots, and the Rescue Homes, and what is there left? "Whoso hath this world's goods, and seeth his brother have need, and shutteth up his bowels of compassion from him, how dwelleth the love of God in him?"

(d) With this love he will love his comrades. In this way they will love him back again. Love begets love.

VI. Nevertheless, with all this sympathy for men and goodness, the Officer possessed of this Burning Love will be a fierce hater of evil. His love of God and truth and righteousness will make him the uncompromising opponent of sin. The more he loves God the more he will hate the Devil. He will not try to serve God and Mammon. The more he loves purity, the more he will hate filthiness. His love of goodness will so educate him into the understanding of the hellish character of badness, and so inflame his heart with hatred of it, that at the Last Day he will consent, nay, rejoice in the everlasting banishment from God of those who will persevere in wickedness. Love and hate are of the same burning spirit.

VII. But, in conjunction with this hatred of evil, the Officer in whose bosom Burning Love reigns will have compassion on evil-doers. In the bosom of Jesus Christ there dwelt the deepest hatred of evil. And yet we read that when He beheld the multitude He had compassion on them. When, from the brow of Olivet, He beheld the men whose hearts were so mastered with evil, and so bitter in their hatred of the Son of God that they resolved to murder Him, He wept over them. When He looked down upon them in His last agony on the bloody Cross to which they had nailed Him, He prayed for their salvation, and broke His heart on their behalf.

Here is an example for us, my comrades. You and I may condemn wickedness. We must condemn it. We cannot help but condemn and hate the drunkenness, the pride, the selfishness, the lust, and a thousand other devilish things that are carried on around us. But if we are possessed of this Burning Love we shall have compassion on the guilty doers of these hateful things.

Where this Burning Love dwells in the heart of an Officer it will carry him out to look on the sinners in their homes, drink shops, haunts of vice. He will look at them as they sit before him in his Halls. His soul will go out after them. He will say of one: Think of his birth, parentage, prayerless mother, swearing father, the example of his home. Oh, my God! how I pity him! Can I help him? Of another he will say: Oh, think of his bringing up; the school-fellows, and the filthy, lying ways they taught him almost before he knew his alphabet! Oh, my God! is the devilry we see in him today to be wondered at? Can I help him?

Of another he will say: Oh, remember his ignorance! How little he knows about God, and sin, and judgment, and Heaven and Hell! And how much less he believes.

Of another he will say: Just look at his temptations, from workmates, publicans, recreations, and devils.

Of another he will say: The inconsistencies of such Christians, parsons, perhaps Salvationists, as he has met with, they have blighted him.

Of another he will say: Oh, remember his failures! How often he has tried. They have given up counting the times he has been to the penitent-form. Weeping at the mercy-seat one night; mocking with his mates, or rolling drunk to his home the next. Poor wretch! O God! how I pity him. What can I do to help him?

Of another: Think of his misery, his wretched health, his comfortless home.

Of yet another: Think of his cantankerous nature, his natural "cussedness," his rebellious or wobbling nature and feeble will. Again, think of that man's coming doom. He will be in Hell soon! And then there will come the reflection: "What might I not have been had I been circumstanced and tempted as these poor sinners and backsliders have been!" As John Bradford said when he saw a criminal being led to execution: "But for the grace of God, there goes John Bradford."

VIII. This Burning Love will make the Officer in whose bosom it dwells not only compassionate, but willing to suffer on behalf of the evil-doers. A willingness to suffer on behalf of those whom you love is inseparable from all true affection. You will find plenty of examples of this even among the creatures whose love is really only instinct, as it is in the animal creation. You will find more in man with his ordinary instinct.

(a) What wonderful things a mother's love, will make her do and suffer! No hardship is counted too great.

(b) What marvels the love of the patriot will accomplish! How willingly, eagerly, the love of country has carried them to deeds of daring, suffering, and death. How the Japanese have gone singing and triumphantly shouting to certain destruction. Consecration signed in blood! But this love is better than the love of kindred, and country, and friends, which has ordinarily some selfish interest behind it. Burning Love unselfishly suffers for its own enemies, and for those whom it knows to be the foes of God and man.

(i.) It was this Burning Love that carried the prophets of old through hardships and suffering and death. Read the history of Moses and the account of God's heroes in the Epistle to the Hebrews.

(ii.) It was this Burning Love that carried Jesus Christ to the Cross.

(iii.) It was this Burning Love that carried the Apostles and martyrs on to their end.

(iv.) It was this Burning Love that carried millions and millions more since that day to a triumphant finish.

(v.) This Burning Love will make Officers preach, pray, visit, deal with difficulties in their Corps, and go to the end of the earth to save souls.

IX. Burning Love will make the Officer the beloved of-

1. Comrades. How Officers complain about their comrades. Some are not loved. Why? Is it not because the Officer has not sufficiently loved them?
2. Those for whom he lights. The weak, the afflicted, the children.
3. God and the angels. Ministering spirits will attend him in his labours.

X. Burning Love will ensure the Officer's perseverance. While this love burns, no fear of retreat.

XI. Burning Love will crown the Officer with glory in the world to come. Celestial rewards will not be according to:

1. Gifts, talents, brilliance of intellect, etc.
2. The number and magnitude of the miracles wrought on the earth.
3. The number of souls won.
4. But according to the measure of love. "She loved much." "Love never faileth: but whether there be prophecies, they shall fail;

whether there be tongues, they shall cease; whether there be knowledge, it shall vanish away... And now abideth faith, hope, love, these three; but the greatest of these is love." That is the standard by which God measures the value of your service on earth, and by which He will measure your reward in Heaven.

XII. Burning Love, the most precious of all gifts, is within the reach of all. The human gifts counted of most value by men are denied to many. All cannot excel in the gift of praying or talking. But all can have the Spirit of Burning Love.

END

For hundreds of other excellent titles see:

www.**Classic**_Christian_**Ebooks**.com

Inspiring and uplifting classics from authors such as:

E. M. Bounds
Amy Carmichael
Alfred Edersheim
Jonathan Edwards
Charles Finney
D. L. Moody
G. Campbell Morgan
Andrew Murray
George Muller
Charles Spurgeon
Hudson Taylor
R. A. Torrey
John Wesley
…and many more!